I Can't Help Praising the Lord

I Can't Help Praising the Lord

The Life of Billy Bray

From *The King's Son* by FW Bourne
Edited and updated by Chris Wright
with additional words from Billy Bray

© Chris Wright 2018

This paperback ISBN: 978-1-912529-00-1

Also available as an eBook
eBook ISBN: 978-1-912529-01-8

The Journal of Billy Bray has been transcribed by Chris Wright and the sections here are reproduced by courtesy and permission of the Director and Librarian of John Rylands University of Manchester and the Methodist Church of Great Britain.

All rights reserved. Without limiting the rights under copyright reserved above, no part of this publication may be reproduced, stored in a retrieval system, or transmitted, in any form or by any means (electronic, mechanical, photocopying, recording or otherwise), without the prior written permission of the copyright owner of this edition.

Published by
White Tree Publishing
Bristol
UNITED KINGDOM
www.whitetreepublishing.com

In conjunction with
The Billy Bray Memorial Trust
www.billybray.org.uk

Three Eyes Chapel Kerley Downs after the extension circa 1860, viewed from the north.

Introduction

"I can't help praising the Lord!" said Billy Bray. "As I go along the street I lift up one foot, and it seems to say 'Glory!' and I lift up the other, and it seems to say 'Amen'; and so they keep on like that all the time I am walking."

Billy was a tin miner by trade and he loved his native Cornwall, but his love for souls was greater. When he was criticized for building a new chapel he replied, "If this new chapel ... stands one hundred years, and one soul be converted in it every year, that will be one hundred souls – and one soul is worth more than all Cornwall!"

Billy Bray (1794-1868) found a real excitement in his Christian life, and discovered the secret of living by faith. His outspoken comments are often amusing, but the reader will be challenged by their directness.

This book has a strong message of encouragement for Christians today. Billy believed and accepted the promises in the Bible, and lived a life that was Spirit filled.

FW Bourne, the writer of the original book, *The King's Son*, knew Billy Bray as a friend. In it he has used Billy's own writing, the accounts of others who had met Billy, and his own memories.

Chris Wright has revised and edited FW Bourne's book to produce this new edition, adding sections directly from Billy Bray's own handwritten *Journal*, keeping Billy's rough and ready grammar and wording, which surely helps us picture this amazing man of God.

Editor's Note

The King's Son by FW Bourne has accounts by three main writers: FW Bourne, Billy Bray and William Haslam. The words of Billy Bray in this edition (in italics) are taken directly from Billy's *Journal*, using Billy's own words rather than Bourne's quotes in which he often corrected Billy's grammar and made "polished" changes to the wording. William Haslam's words (also in italics) are from his book *From Death into Life*. My own occasional comments are within square brackets [thus]. Everything in standard type is taken from Bourne's 1877 edition of *The King's Son*.

Bourne's first edition of *The King's Son*, dated 1871, three years after Billy's death, was a small volume in which he asked his readers for their memories of Billy Bray. Note that Bourne has written *The King's Son* under various subject headings, rather than putting events in chronological order.

The complete *Journal* of Billy Bray (approximately 49,000 words) which I transcribed word by word from the original, is in my book *Billy Bray in His Own Words*, published by Highland Books.

An abridged edition of Williams Haslam's two-volume autobiography, *From Death Into Life* and *Yet Not I*, is available as an eBook from White Tree Publishing in most formats entitled *Haslam's Journey*. ISBN: 978-1-9997899-9-2.

Chris Wright

Contents

1. Billy's Conversion 1
2. The First-Fruits Of Harvest 7
3. Joy Unspeakable and Full of Glory 16
4. Chapel Building 25
5. The Prayer of Faith 45
6. Pure Religion 50
7. Sabbath Keeping 54
8. Trials and Conflicts 59
9. Drinking and Smoking 65
10. Rebuke and Exhortation 70
11. Fully Ripe for the Garner 73

Chapter 1

Billy's Conversion

Therefore if any man be in Christ, he is a new creature: old things are passed away; behold, all things are become new (2 Corinthians 5:17).

When God enters our lives we are changed. Saul of Tarsus was changed, transformed from a persecutor of Christians to become the renowned Apostle of the Gentiles. A blaspheming tinker of Bedford, John Bunyan, was changed into a much loved writer and preacher. It was the same grace that changed Billy Bray, formerly a drunken miner, into a loving and consistent disciple of the Son of God.

[Billy writes in his *Journal*:] *My grandfather was one of the old Methodists, for he joined them when Mister Wesley first came to Cornwall. He was my father's father. My father died when we was young, and left my mother with five small children. After father died, grandfather took us to rear. He could not read a letter in the book, but I have heard him [my grandfather] say, "We must be born again, and I was born again up in our croft among the furze [gorse]. I was so happy I could tell the bushes to praise God. I thought I was in a new world."*

My grandfather, and a few more that was converted when he was, built a little chapel in a place called Twelveheads. There was a special little class, and they had a leader called Sando.

I write to honour my God. You will not wonder how I praise him when you read what he has done for me, bless his Holy Name.

I was born in the parish of Kea in the county of Cornwall in June 1794. My father died when I was about eight years old and, as I have already said, my grandfather reared me. I lived in Cornwall until I was seventeen years old, and then I went up to Devonshire and there I lived a bad life.

Once, I was working underground, and I heard a scat [a break] overhead. I ran out, and, I think, forty tons fell down where I had been working but a minute before.

Billy had not yet reached the lowest depths of evil and misery. Turned away from the tin mine at which he worked, for being insolent to the mine captain, he moved to another part of Devonshire, and went to live at an alehouse.

There, with other drunkards, I drank all night long. But I had a sore head and a sick stomach, and worse than all, horrors of mind that no tongue can tell. I used to dread to go to sleep for fear of waking up in hell; and though I made many promises to the Lord to be better, I was soon as bad or worse than ever. After being absent from my native county seven years, I returned a drunkard.

I was not only a drunkard but bad in other ways, and it is too bad to put down here. Great was the mercy of God towards me or I should not be here, bless and praise his Holy Name for what he done for me in delivering my soul from the pit.

One time I remember I went for some coal that my wife sent me for. I got the coal, and there was a beer shop in the way, and there I stayed. I got drunk, and my poor wife was forced to come for me and wheel home the coal herself.

John Bunyan, when he was in the prison writing the Visions of Heaven and Hell, *he did not know the Lord would make him instrumental in converting my soul. But he was, and I bless the Lord that ever John Bunyan was put in prison. Bless his Holy Name that little book called* Bunyan's Visions of Heaven and Hell *was brought into our house. Who brought it there I do not know. Bless the Lord for sending of it there. I took it in my hand and began to read it.*

When I was sitting down to the end of the table reading the book, my wife was sitting by the fire. She had been converted when young but she went back before we went together, so she was a backslider. I asked her what it was to be happy. [Here and elsewhere, being happy is Billy's way of describing someone having a true Christian faith.]

I Can't Help Praising The Lord

She said, "No tongue can tell what they enjoy that serve the Lord."

Then I said, "Why don't you begin again? I may begin too." I thought if she was to begin it would be better for me, for I was ashamed to go to my knees to pray before her that very night. I felt in my mind that I ought to fall on my knees and ask God for mercy, but the devil had such a hold in me that he made me ashamed [to pray in front] of my wife.

I went into bed without prayer, and it was about ten o'clock at night. At three in the morning, I think, I awaked and thought about what I read the night before. I thought, if I stay until my wife is converted I may never be saved.

Then I rose out of the bed and went to my knees for the first time. My wife heard me but she could not see me for it was dark. Bless and praise the Lord, I have never been ashamed of [praying in front of] my wife since that night, and there is forty years gone since that time.

That very day I made up my mind to serve the Lord by his help, and I began to pray. It was on a Friday, but what day of November it was I do not know. The more I prayed, the more I felt to pray. It was our payday or setting day that day, I hardly know which, for it is a long time ago.

I stayed upstairs all the forenoon asking the Lord to have mercy upon me, and in the afternoon I went to the alehouse to meet with my comrades, the men I work with. We always went, we miners, on setting days and paydays to the alehouse to eat and to drink, and to get drunk and to tell lies [jokes]. I was the worse liar of the whole, and their chairman among them.

We was eight men that worked together. When I came in among them they looked at me, and they knew that I was not like I was some time before. Yes, they had lost their chairman, and one of them swore.

I said to him, "We must give account of that one day."

Mocking me, he said, "Shall us go to the Bryanites [Bible Christians] meeting?"

I said, "It is better to go there than go to hell."

I came home that night sober the first time for many years, for we always got drunk on our setting day and

3

payday. My wife was greatly surprised to see me come home so soon, and sober too. She said, "How are you home so soon today?"

I said unto her, "You will never see me drunk no more, by the help of the Lord."

And she never have since, praise the Lord. The Lord can, and do, cure drunken wicked men, praise his Holy Name. That night I went upstairs and prayed until we went to bed. The next day I did not go to work. I took the Bible and Wesley's hymnbook and went up the stairs into the bedroom. This was the Saturday, and there I read and prayed all the day. Sometimes I read the Bible and then the hymnbook, and then asked the Lord for mercy.

When Sunday morning came it was very wet. There was a class meeting a mile from our house, called Bible Christians. I went to the house where the meeting was held, but because it was wet none of them came. I had a mind to meet with them, but when I saw a little rain would keep them from the house of God, I said, "I shall not meet here if a drop of rain will keep them home."

This hasty decision was soon reversed, for Billy was a consistent member with the Bible Christians for more than forty years, and died in communion with the people of his early choice. But how much harm such lukewarm Christians do to inquirers after salvation and to young converts, it is impossible to determine.

I went home from the meeting house, went up to our bedroom, and took the Bible and hymnbook again. Sometimes I read, and then prayed, and asked the Lord to have mercy on me. I felt the devil very busy with me, and he tempted me that I should never find mercy. But I never believed him, for I knew that the Lord said. "All that seek shall find." And that is true, bless his Holy Name for ever and ever.

On the Monday I was all the forepart of the day in my bedroom, some of the time reading, and then asking the Lord for mercy. Then I had to go to the mine, for we was afternoon core. We went down underground, four of us, and went to work. While working, I was always asking the Lord to have mercy on me. The men that I worked with me was wisht [upset] to see me so, for I used to tell lies to make them laugh. But now I was not like Billy Bray, for last week I was a servant of the devil, and now I was determined to serve the Lord, by his help. And I believed he would help me.

My wife's mother told me I must not be out of heart if I did not find God's mercy in twelve months. I told her I should not be so long as that, though the devil tempted me hard that I should never find it. Thanks be to the Lord I found him a liar. I was glad that I had begun to seek the Lord, for I would rather be crying for mercy than living in sin.

At that time we had a little pig, and this was the Wednesday. While in the bedroom looking to heaven with all the powers of my soul, it appeared to me I had almost laid hold of the blessing. But the pig came up to our door and I thought I never heard a pig cry so in all my life. I should have been very glad if some person had drive him away, if I never saw him no more.

I did not get the blessing then, though it seem so nigh me. By the devil and the pig, I got it not then: with the pig downstairs crying and the devil tempting. For want of a little more faith I got not the blessing, and it was come time for me to go work to the mine.

When I came home I went upstairs, not staying for supper, for I wanted something better. And bless God I soon had it. I stayed up in my bedroom with my face to the west, and I said to the dear Lord, "Thou hast said they that ask shall receive, and they that seek shall find, and they that knock it shall be opened unto them. Open unto me, my dear Lord. I have faith to believe it."

When I said so, the dear Lord made me so happy that I cannot express what I felt. I shouted for joy and praised God for what he had done for me a poor sinner, for I could say my happy heart felt experience that the Lord had pardoned all my sins. And it seem to me I was in a new world. I think it was in November 1823. What day of the month I do not know, but everything looked new to me: the people, the fields, the cattle, the trees. I was like a man in a new world.

Glory be to God, I was so happy that I was the greatest part of my time praising the Lord. I could say, "O Lord, I will praise thee, for thou wast angry with me but thine anger is turned away, and thou comforts me." Or like David, "The Lord brought me out of the horrible pit and mire and clay, and set my feet on the rock, established my goings, and put a new song in my mouth of praise and thanks given to God."

I was a new man altogether. All that I met I told what the Lord had done for my soul. I heard some say that they have hard work to get away from their old companions, but I had hard work to find them, for I was glad to meet them to tell them what the Lord had done for me.

Some said I was mad, and some said, "We shall have him again next payday."

I always got drunk on our mine payday, and they thought I should go back again. But praise the Lord, there is more than forty years gone and they have not got me yet. They said I was a mad man, but they meant I was a glad man, and I have been glad ever since. Bless and praise his Holy Name for what he have done for we poor sinners that was once servants of the devil and now are the servants of the Lord; once in the road to hell but now in the road to heaven."

Billy Bray's house at Twelveheads

Chapter 2

The First-Fruits of Harvest

Billy Bray's wife, Joanna (Joey), was the first to yield to his entreaties, and about a week afterwards in Hicks Mill Chapel she regained the blessing she had lost. Billy had spent much of his time in his unconverted state in telling lies to "make fun", as his companions called it; "but now I could tell them a new tale about heavenly truths, and what the Lord had done for me."

This was not so pleasing to many; but *"Bless and praise his Holy Name, I never shall forget the day when Jesus took my sins away."*

[But not all Billy's friends are pleased to hear what has happened. Billy continues:] *In the day of Pentecost, they that was not converted said the Lord's children was drunk with new wine. It was not long before some of the men was as mad as me. There were men that professed to be converted before I was, but did not love their Lord well enough to honour him in the mine, and did not love we well enough to tell us that the Lord would make us happy. They never prayed with me, nor told me that I must pray or go to hell. But when I was converted, the Lord gave me power to tell all that I met with that I was happy and was going to heaven. I told them that what the Lord had done for me, he would do for everyone that ask him.*

There was no one that prayed in our mine where I worked, but when the Lord converted my soul I used to pray underground with the men before we go to our different places to work. Sometimes I felt it a heavy cross, but the cross is the way to the crown. Sometimes I have had as many as six to ten men down with me, and I have said to them, "Now if you will hearken to me, I will pray for you before we go to work. For," I said, "if I do not pray for you before we go to work, and anyone be killed, I should think it was my fault."

Some of them would say, "You pray and we will hear you."

Then I should pray in what the people call simple words, and in the way that I hope the Lord would have me. I used say when praising God, "If anyone must be killed or die today, let me. Do not let no one of them die, for they are not happy, but I am. And I shall be in heaven if I die today."

When I did rise from my knees I should see the tears running down their faces. Soon after, some of them became praying men themselves.

The Rev. William Haslam was converted dramatically [while preaching his own sermon at nearby Baldhu!]. He wrote [to Bourne]: "In the heyday of my prosperity, and in the success of my sacramental ministrations, while I thought the Church was the ark — and no salvation could be had outside the Church, except by some unconvenanted mercy — one of my most promising disciples, a regular communicant and zealous Churchman, was taken seriously ill.

[This, and subsequent quotes in italics by William Haslam are from his book *From Death into Life*, rather than Bourne's version of it.]

At that time my gardener, a good Churchman who was duly despised by his neighbours for attaching himself to me and my teaching, fell seriously ill. I sent him at once to the doctor, who pronounced him to be in a miner's consumption and gave no hope of his recovery. No sooner did my gardener realise his position and see eternity before him, than all the Church teaching I had given him failed to console or satisfy. His heart sank within him at the near prospect of death.

In his distress of mind he did not send for me to come and pray with him, but actually sent for a converted man who lived in the next row of cottages. This man, instead of building him up, as I had done, went to work in the opposite direction — to show my servant that he was a lost sinner and needed to come to Jesus, just as he was, for pardon and salvation. He was brought under deep conviction of sin, and eventually found peace through the precious blood of Jesus.

I Can't Help Praising The Lord

Immediately it spread all over the parish that, "The Parson's servant is converted!" The news soon reached me, but instead of giving joy it brought the most bitter disappointment and sorrow to my heart. I felt hurt to think that after all I had taught him against schism he should fall into so great an error. However, he sent for me again and again, till at last his entreaties prevailed and I went. Instead of lying on his bed, a dying man as I expected to find him, he was walking about the room in a most joyful and ecstatic state.

"Oh, dear master," he exclaimed, "I am glad you are come. I am so happy. My soul is saved. Glory be to God!"

"Come, John," I said, "sit down and be quiet, and I will have a talk with you and tell you what I think."

But John knew my thoughts well enough, so he burst out, "Oh, master, I am sure you do not know about this, or you would have told me. I am quite sure you love me, and I love you, that I do. But, dear master, you do not know this. I am praying for the Lord to show it to you. I mean to pray till I die, and after that if I can, till you are converted."

He looked at me so lovingly, and seemed so truly happy, that it was more than I could stand. Almost involuntarily I made for the door and escaped before he could stop me.

I went home greatly disturbed in my mind, altogether disappointed and disgusted with my work among these Cornish people, thinking, "It is no use, they never will be Churchmen."

I was as hopeless and miserable as I could be. I felt that my superior teaching and practice had failed, and that the inferior and, as I believed, unscriptural dogmas had prevailed. My favourite and most promising Churchman had fallen — and was happy in his fall. More than that, he was actually praying that I might fall too!

Like the elder brother of the Prodigal Son I was grieved, and even angry, because he was restored to favour and joy. Nothing seemed to give me any rest in this crisis of my parochial work. I thought I would give up my parish and church, and go and work in some more congenial soil. Or else that I would preach a set of sermons on the subject of schism, for perhaps I had not sufficiently taught my people the danger of this great sin.

Every parishioner I passed seemed to look at me as if to say, "So much for your teaching. You will never convince us!"

Mr Haslam's heart was now "broken for work." A visit to a brother clergyman [Rev. Robert Aitken at Pendeen] deepened his convictions, for he plainly told him that if he had been converted he would have rejoiced in that man's salvation and praised God with him, and that he would never do any good in his parish until he was converted himself.

So deep became Mr. Haslam's distress that, when the bell tolled for service on the following Sunday morning, he trembled and feared to preach; but while preaching on the words *What think ye of Christ?* the Lord showed him so clearly that Christ was the true and only foundation, the Lamb of God that taketh away the sin of the world, that his soul was filled with joy, "as full of joy as it had been of misery!" The fervour and earnestness with which he now proclaimed "a present salvation", caused a general cry for mercy, and many of his parishioners were saved. It was no wonder that Billy wished to see him, *to give his eyes a treat,* as he said, and to witness some of the blessed results of his prayer of faith years before.

William Haslam suddenly realises the truth of what he is preaching, and a visiting preacher stands up and shouts, "Halleluiah, the parson is converted!"

I Can't Help Praising The Lord

[Three years (Bourne says three months) after his conversion while preaching his own sermon, William Haslam writes,] *When all the people on the hill where the church was built were converted, there came upon the scene a very remarkable person who had evidently been kept back for a purpose. This was none other than the veritable and well-known Billy Bray. One morning while we were sitting at breakfast I heard someone walking about in the hall with a heavy step, saying, "Praise the Lord! Praise the Lord!"*

On opening the door I beheld a happy-looking little man in a black Quaker-cut coat which it was very evident had not been made for him, but for some much larger body.

"Well, my friend," I said, "who are you?"

"I am Billy Bray," he replied, looking steadily at me with his twinkling eyes. "And be you the passon?"

"Yes, I am."

"Thank the Lord. Converted, are ye?"

"Yes, thank God."

"And the missus inside?" He pointed to the dining room. "Be she converted?"

"Yes, she is."

"Thank the dear Lord," he said, moving forward.

I made way for him and he came stepping into the room. Then making a profound bow to the said "missus", he asked, "Be there any maidens?" He meant servants.

"Yes, there are three in the kitchen."

"Be they converted too?"

I was able to answer in the affirmative, and as I pointed towards the kitchen door when I mentioned it, he made off in that direction. Soon we heard them all shouting, and praising God together.

When we went in, there was Billy Bray very joyful, singing, "Canaan is a happy place, I am bound for the land of Canaan!"

We returned to the dining room with our strange guest, when he suddenly caught me up in his arms and carried me round the room. I was so taken by surprise that it was as much as I could do to keep myself in an upright position till he had accomplished the circuit. Then he set me in my chair, and rolling on the ground for joy, said that he was "as happy as he could live."

When this performance was at an end he rose with a face that was beaming all over. I invited him to take some breakfast with us, to which he assented with thanks. He chose bread and milk, for he said, "I am only a child." I asked him to be seated and gave him a chair, but he preferred walking about, and went on talking all the time. He told us that twenty years ago as he was walking over this very hill on which my church and house were built — it was a barren old place then — the Lord said to him, "I will give thee all that dwell in this mountain."

Immediately he fell down on his knees and thanked the Lord, and then ran to the nearest cottage. There he talked and prayed with the people, and was enabled to bring them to Christ. Then he went to the next cottage and got the same blessing, and then to a third where he was equally successful. Then he told "Father" that there were only three "housen" in this mountain, and prayed that more might be built. That prayer remained with him, and he never ceased to make it for years. The neighbours who heard his prayer from time to time wondered why he should ask for "housen" to be built in such an "ungain" place.

At last, after sixteen years, he received a letter from his brother James to say that they were hacking up the croft to plant trees, and that they were going to build a church on the hill. He was "fine and glad" and praised the Lord. Again he did so when his brother wrote to say there was a Vicarage to be built on the same hill, and a schoolroom also. He was almost beside himself with joy and thankfulness for all this.

In the year 1848, when the church was completed and opened, he came on a visit to Baldhu and was greatly surprised to see what a change had taken place. There was a beautiful church, a Parsonage with a flourishing garden, and a schoolroom, with a large plantation and fields round them.

He was quite "mazed" for he never thought that the old hill could be made so grand as that. However, when he went to the service in the church, his joy was over. He came out "checkfallen" and quite disappointed. He told "Father" *that that was nothing but an "old Pusey" [Haslam!] he had got there, and that he was no good. While he was praying that afternoon, "Father" gave him to understand that he had no business there yet, and that he had come too soon and without permission. So he went back to his place at once, near Bodmin, and continued to pray for the hill.*

After three years his brother James wrote again. This time it was to tell him that the Parson and all his family were converted, and that there was a great revival at the church. Now poor Billy was most eager to come and see this for himself, but he obtained no permission, though he asked and looked for it every day for more than three months.

At last, one wintry and frosty night in January, about half-past eleven as he was getting into bed, "Father" told him that he might go to Baldhu. He was so overjoyed that he did not wait till the morning, but immediately "put up" his clothes again, "hitched in" the donkey and set out in his slow-going little cart. He came along singing all the way, nearly thirty miles, and arrived early in the morning. Having put up his donkey in my stable he came into the house and presented himself in the hall, praising God, as I have already stated.

We were a long time over breakfast that morning, for the happy man went on from one thing to another, "telling of the Lord" as he called it, assuring us again and again that he was "fine and glad, and very happy." Indeed, he looked so. He said there was one thing more he must tell us. It was this: that he had a preaching-house, what we should now call a mission-room, which he had built years ago. He had often prayed there for "this old mountain" and now he should dearly love to see me in the pulpit of that place, and said that he would let me have it for my work.

As the Rev. MG Pearse says, "If you had joined Billy on the way, you could not have been long in doubt as to who he was. A little, spare, wiry man, whose dress of orthodox black, and the white tie, indicated the preacher. The sharp, quick, discerning eye that looked out from under the brows, the mouth almost hard in its decision, all the face softened by the light that played constantly upon it, and by the happy wrinkles round the eyes, and the smile that had perpetuated itself — these belonged to no ordinary man. And with the first suspicion that this was Billy Bray there would quickly come enough to confirm it. If you gave him half a chance there would certainly be a straightforward question about your soul, in wise pithy words. And if the answer was what it should be, the lanes would ring with his happy thanksgiving."

I [Bourne] remember once hearing Billy speak with great effect to a large congregation, principally miners. In that neighbourhood there were two mines — one very prosperous, where good wages could be earned; but at the other the work was hard, and the wages low. He represented himself to the congregation as working at *that* mine, but on the payday going to the prosperous one for his wages! But had he not been at work at the other mine, the manager would inquire? He had, but he liked the wages at the good mine the best. Billy continued to act out this 'play' to the congregation. He pleaded very earnestly, but in vain. He was dismissed at last with the remark, from which there was no appeal, that he must come there to *work* if he came there for his *wages*. And then he turned upon the congregation, and the effect was almost irresistible: they must serve Christ here if they would share his glory hereafter, but if they would serve the devil now, to him they must go for their wages by-and-by.

At such times Billy would generally express his determination to live up to his glorious privileges, and enjoy the varied *abundance* of his Father's house. Some could only eat out of the *silent* dish, but he could eat out of that, and also out of the *shouting* dish, and *jumping* dish, and every other; or, as he sometimes put it, "I can say glory, glory. I can *sing* glory, glory. I can *dance* glory, glory," generally accompanying the word with the act.

He was one of the preachers at the opening of the new chapel at Lake, near Shebbear, famed as being the birthplace of the Bible Christian Connexion. SL Thorne informs us that Billy's text was: "Behold, we have forsaken all, and followed thee: what shall we have therefore?" and that he contrasted

I Can't Help Praising The Lord

Peter with his nets and fish in his boat, and Peter upon a throne in glory; and he thought Peter had every reason to be pleased with his reward.

There was great excitement and much apparent confusion in some of Billy's meetings, more than sufficient to shock the prejudices of the highly sensitive. Billy could not tolerate "deadness", as he expressively called it, either in a professing Christian or in a meeting. He had a deep sympathy with people singing, or shouting or leaping for joy.

His services were distasteful only to a few, and many prejudiced hearers were soon convinced that his method was right or, influenced and attracted by the simplicity and warmth, were led to join in heartily. He speaks of John, who worked with him in Devonshire, and returned at the same time to Cornwall. They were also converted together, but while Billy joined the Bible Christians, his companion cast in his lot with the Wesleyan Methodists.

When Billy was appointed to a chapel near where one of his friends, John, lived, John came to hear him but would leave immediately after Billy had done speaking, as he could not enjoy the subsequent proceedings — some singing, some praying, some shouting, some dancing, scenes that were once frequently to be witnessed when the Cornish people got what they called the "victory".

But one Saturday night John had a dream which brought him to the conclusion that he was wrong in opposing shouting when the Lord made his people happy. The next night, and ever afterwards, he stopped until the end of the meeting, and shouted as loudly, and leaped as joyfully as Billy himself. He lived a good life, and died a happy death, Billy remarking at his funeral, "So, he has done with the *doubters,* and is got up with the *shouters!*"

Chapter 3

Joy Unspeakable and Full of Glory

[Billy continues in his *Journal:*] *I was born in the fire and could not live in the smoke, for I was happy in my work and could leap and dance for joy. I could do it in the mine underground, as well as up to the surface.*

My master persecuted me, and would say that it was no religion to leap and dance and make so to-do — there was no need for it. My master, or captain, was down in the mine where I was, and we was working an end, and we had a little water standing in. He began to speak against me, and I looked to the Lord. Then power of the Lord came upon me and I began to jump and smash the water up in his face and his eyes, and put out his candle. He went out shaking his head and asked my comrade, where he hid, "Is this a mad man with thee?"

But he made a mistake. I was not a mad man but I was a glad man, and the Lord made me so, bless his Holy Name. David was not a mad man when he danced before the Lord with all his might, though his wife called him so. She said he was like one of the wild fellows, shameful, uncovered. But he told her he would be more vile yet, for it was before the Lord that he leaped and danced.

It was the Lord that made me so happy as to make me dance and leap for joy. And David's Lord is my Lord, bless his Holy Name. If a man will not leap and dance for heaven, what will he leap and dance for? There is no better prize than heaven, and we are heaven born and heaven bound.

The sinner says, "We think there is no need for as much to-do as to leap and dance and make so much noise, for the Lord is not deaf and he know our hearts."

And you must know that the devil is not deaf neither, yet his servants make a great noise. But the devil would rather see us doubting than hear us shouting. We believe without a doubt that Christians have a right to shout, but

I Can't Help Praising The Lord

the lukewarm professor [a nominal Christian professing the Christian faith] will say there is no need for so much noise.

[A story in Cornwall sums up the gap that existed between the supporters of tranquillity and the advocates of animation in the Cornish chapels and churches. Billy told the Rev. Saltern Rogers, the vicar of Gwennap from 1856-1893, "Look 'ere, Passun Rogers, you do love a peace and quietness religion, but I do dearly love a noise!"]

Billy was once asked, "Why can't you worship the Lord without making so much noise?"

"It's not my fault," said Billy. "If a person above was to pour water into a basin already full, standing on that beautiful tablecloth, and it was splashing all about, you would not blame the basin. You would tell the person to stop pouring the water, as it was splashing all about and you could not enjoy yourselves. I am only the vessel. My Heavenly Father is pouring down the water of life freely, and if you can't bear it, call to him not to pour so much."

[Billy writes:] *One of our preachers said, if I did not stop cocking up my leg he would tell Brother Sedwell of it. And if he would not stop me, he would tell Mister O'Brian of it. And if he would not stop me, he would turn me out of the communion. [Probably Hicks Mill Chapel.]*

I told him to go and tell that gentleman that Brother Sedwell nor Mister O'Brian did not pardon my sins, for Jesus Christ had pardoned my sins and set my soul at liberty. And while he will give me the power, he do know if they cut off my legs I should cock up the stumps — and the dear Lord is able to do so, for there is no limits to his power. For in him there is everlasting strength.

In that blessed name of Jesus Christ, the cripple was made strong in the day of Peter. When he went into the temple, walking and leaping and praising God, the people greatly wondered. But Peter did not tell the lame man that he cock up his leg too high. If a lame man could leap for joy, a man that never was lame ought to leap.

You may say, "It is no wonder for him to leap, for it is a new thing to him." And so it was, and it is new too, for there is no old thing in heaven. It is always new, and the last blessing is the best. Justification is a great blessing, but sanctification is a greater one.

Hick's Mill Chapel

At a district meeting held at Hicks Mill Chapel in 1866, Mr. Oliver, in describing the triumphant death of a woman, said she died shouting "Victory." This touched Billy's heart, and he shouted "Glory! If a *dying* woman praised the Lord, I should think a *living* man might!"

If you did not join him in praising God, Billy would always at once say that he thought you were *dead!* "For is not," said he, "the Lord worthy to be praised from the rising to the setting of the sun? And yet you will not praise him at all!"

I went with him one day to see a dying Christian man, whose holy character had been unblemished for many years, but whose natural disposition was modest and retiring almost to a fault. His face wore a look of dignity and repose, and was lit up with a strange, unearthly radiance and glory. He was just on the verge of heaven. He could only speak in a whisper. He said, "I wish I had a voice, so that I might praise the Lord!"

"You should have praised him, my brother, when you had one!" was Billy's quiet, but slightly satirical comment.

I Can't Help Praising The Lord

We are expressly told that we are "to count it all joy when we fall into divers temptations." So did Billy Bray. He could smile through his tears. The sickness of a child, the death of his wife, were powerless to silence his voice, or to repress his joy. It is said that when his wife died he was so overpowered with the thought of his "dear Joey" having escaped from earth's toils and sufferings to the rest and bliss of heaven, that he began to jump and dance about the room, exclaiming, "Bless the Lord! My dear Joey is gone up with the bright ones! My dear Joey is gone up with the shining angels! Glory! Glory! Glory!"

"Here," Billy would say, "we have a little bitter, but it is mixed with a great deal of sweet. The sinner thinks he is going to give up something very good, in exchange for what is not so good when he comes to Christ."

Mr. CG Honor, a Primitive Methodist minister, says that at a love-feast in their chapel at St. Blazey, when Billy was present, several people spoke of their trials, but said that their blessings more than counterbalanced them. At length Billy rose. Clapping his hands and smiling, he said, "Well, friends, I have been taking vinegar and honey, but praise the Lord, I've had the vinegar with a *spoon,* and the honey with a *ladle.*" He had trials as others, but "it was not worth while to speak or write anything about them."

He was on the road to heaven, and why should he not praise God *every step* of the way? "I would rather *walk* to heaven over the roughest road, with bleeding feet," he often said, "than *ride* to hell even in a fine carriage." But it excites a smile to hear him speak of "showing people *how* we shall walk the golden streets in heaven, and with *golden slippers,* too."

Billy nearly always expressed a wish when he visited the sick and dying, that he might "see them in heaven, dressed in robes of glorious brightness; for," he would add, in his quietest vein of humour, "if I saw them there, *I must be there myself too!*"

If people said he praised God too *loud,* he would point heavenward and say, "Up there we shall praise him more sweet, more *loud";* and sometimes, "If the Lord were to stop my breath this moment I should be with him in glory at once. I have a heaven while going to heaven."

If any man could sing, "Heaven is my home," it was Billy Bray. To a friend in Liskeard, he said, when leaving on one occasion, "I shan't see you many times more, ma'am."

"Why not, Billy?"

"My Heavenly Father will want me home — will be soon sending for me."

Then he was asked: "Do you think we shall know each other in heaven?"

He answered: "Why, missus, do you think we shall be more ignorant in heaven than we are down here. We are not going to spend our time there, saying, 'Who's that over there?' We shall spend our time in singing the song of Moses, the servant of God, and of the Lamb. I shall know Adam as soon as I see him, as if I had been reared with him all my life!"

In a friend's house in Falmouth, he exhorted those present to praise the Lord. Speaking of himself, Billy said, "I can't help praising the Lord! As I go along the street I lift up one foot, and it seems to say 'Glory!' and I lift up the other, and it seems to say 'Amen'; and so they keep on like that all the time I am walking."

On one occasion, when in the Penzance preaching circuit on special work, he slept at a friend's house. Very early in the morning Billy was out of bed, jumping, dancing, and singing the praises of God as usual. His friend said, "Billy, why are you out thus so early? You will disturb the family, and perhaps give offence."

The next moment Billy was again leaping and praising the Lord. Then naming the members of the household, he said that they might lie and sleep and let their wheels get rusty if they liked, but he would see to it that his wheels were kept nicely oiled, and ready for work! Then he fell on his knees and prayed aloud for the members of the family, while his prayer for his host was that the Lord would have mercy on him, and make him a better man than he appears to be!

[Writing about preachers who wanted people to stay quiet in chapel, Billy says:] *There was a preacher in a chapel one day and his text was, "Quench not the Spirit." So he*

I Can't Help Praising The Lord

preached away from this text, but he was a bad hypocrite and the Lord never sent him there. These sort of preachers can talk well. He said a great many good things about the Spirit, and there was many happy people in the chapel that knew about the Spirit. They was glad to hear about the Spirit, for the Spirit of the Lord was their best friend, for he was their all and in all.

They came for the very purpose to meet with the Spirit, and the Spirit and the Lord was there. But not for that preacher. He drew nigh the Lord with his lips, when his heart was far away. We that is happy should think that this preacher gave great encouragement to we shouting and dancing Christians, but the tree is known by his fruit.

When he was preaching and telling so much about the Spirit, one of our sisters felt so much of that happy Spirit that she shouted and praised the Lord with a loud voice. We should think that our sister would please the preacher, but she did not. And the reason was that he had not that Spirit himself.

Reader, you may ask, "How do you know that the preacher had not the Spirit?" Because he told the people to quench not the Spirit, and then he told them to quench the Spirit.

Then the preacher said, "I wish that woman would keep silence there."

And that good sister, to please him, quench the Spirit for the time. So the preacher preached away from "Quench not the Spirit." Then the same sister felt so much of that blessed Spirit that she was forced to praise God with a loud voice. So did another sister, and a brother, that the dear Lord made so happy and gave them as much of that blessed Spirit that the preacher was telling about. They shouted aloud for joy, all three of them, and praised the Lord with loud voices.

The preacher that preached from "Quench not the Spirit" was very poor tempered because they done what he told them to do, but he meant for them to quench the Spirit all the time. As soon as they began to shout, he got angry with them, and he would not preach any more. A good brother that belong to that chapel, that lead the class, gave out a hymn and they sang. Then he prayed for the Lord to convert the preacher.

Now that class leader was a converted man and knew what he was telling of, for he was born twice: once of the flesh and once of the Spirit. He and his class could say, "Lord, I will praise thee, for thou once was angry with us but thine anger is turned away, and thou comforts us." They could say with John Wesley, "Oh for a thousand tongues to sing, my great Redeemer's praise!"

That preacher would make a poor companion for John Wesley, for John Wesley wanted a thousand tongues to praise God with: that was nine hundred and ninety-nine tongues more than he had. He wanted to praise the dear Lord, and he wanted to spread the name of the Lord all over the earth. And he wanted a thousand tongues to do it.

So John Wesley loved to hear the name of the dear Lord praised. If that preacher did not love to hear the name of the dear Lord praised, there is many of the Methodists that do — and he would too, was he happy. These sort of preachers will find themselves under a great mistake when they come to die.

Sometimes when Billy quoted the line, "Oh, for a thousand tongues to sing!" he would say, "But many of you don't sing with the *one* tongue you have. A bird that *can* sing, and *won't* sing, ought to be *made* to sing;" and if anyone objected to his singing he would say, "Wesley wanted nine hundred and ninety-nine tongues more than *he* had, and it is very hard if Billy Bray cannot use his *one!*" By such remarks he frequently made them feel ashamed at their having opposed, even playfully, the joyous saint.

[In the Shaw Collection, in the Courtney Library at the Royal Institution of Cornwall in Truro, there is a revealing fragment someone has copied from the records of an unnamed preaching circuit:]

Local Preachers Minutes 1855 — that Brother Bray's name come on the plan as an accredited local preacher.

Quarterly Meeting 1857 — that William Bray be informed that the meeting is grieved by his having allowed

an unauthorised person to preach in his stead and that he is desired not to do so again.
Local Preachers Plan March 1858 — that William Bray's resignation be received.
Quarterly Meeting September 1858 — that William Bray, Bible Christian local preacher, be not allowed to take any active part in our public services.
[This is almost certainly the result of a falling out with the local circuit leaders, a not uncommon event at this time for many preachers. Note how Brother Bray becomes William Bray, and he is finally identified beyond any possible doubt!]

Mr. Gilbert says that he spent an hour or two with Billy in the evening. I told him that I had seen his mother at Twelveheads, and that I found her in a very blessed frame of mind, and that whilst I was praying with her she became so happy that, although quite blind, she jumped and danced about the house, shouting the praises of God! Billy at once became much excited and, rising from his chair, began to dance also.

He then said, "Dear old soul! Dance, did she? I am glad to hear that. Bless the Lord! Well, I dance sometimes. Why shouldn't I dance as well as David! David, you say, was a king; well, bless the Lord, *I* am a King's son! I have as good a right to dance as David had. Bless the Lord! I get very happy at times; my soul gets full of the glory, and then I dance too! I was home in my room t'other day, and I got so happy that I danced, and the glory came streaming down upon my soul, and it made me dance so lustily that my heels went down through the planchen [floorboards]."

Mr. Robins informs me that at a chapel anniversary Billy once said: "I went in to Truro to buy a frock for my little daughter, and coming home I felt very happy, and got catching up my heels a little bit, and I danced the frock out of the basket. When I came home, my wife Joey said, 'William, where's the frock?' I said, 'I don't know, isn't it in the basket?' 'No,' said Joey. 'Glory be to God,' I said, 'I danced the frock out of the basket.'

"The next morning I went to the class meeting, and one was speaking of his trials, and another was speaking of *his* trials, and I said, 'I've got trials too, for yesterday I went into Truro and bought a frock for my little girl. Coming home I got catching up my heels a little bit, and I danced the frock out of the basket.' So they gave me the money I had paid for the frock; and two or three days afterwards someone picked up the frock and brought it to me; so I had two frocks for one. Glory!" and he closed his narration with one of his favourite sayings when anyone opposed and persecuted him for singing and shouting so much, "If they were to put me into a barrel, I would shout glory out through the bunghole! Praise the Lord!"

The Rev. SW Christophers says, I remember somebody saying to Billy as he sat at a friend's table, "How long should I pray at a time, Billy, to keep my soul healthy!" "Do'e see that there piece of brass?" Billy replied, pointing to a polished ornament on the chimney-piece. "If you give that five minutes' rub every now and then you'll keep it bright; but if you let 'im go a long time without it, you will have a long rub to get 'im bright again."

Chapter 4

Chapel Building

Probably no part of England [in the nineteenth century], is better supplied with places of religious worship than the county of Cornwall. The great majority of these have been built by the self-denying efforts of the poor rather than by the encouragement and generosity of the wealthier classes. The people generally put their shoulder to the wheel, and preferred to help themselves rather than be dependent on the charity of others — they trusted almost wholly to God's blessing on their own exertions.

[Billy writes:] *In the neighbourhood where I lived there were a great many dark-minded, wicked people, and chapels were few. The Lord put it into my mind to build a chapel. My mother had some land, and by one of her little fields there was a small piece of open ground. The Lord opened my mother's heart to give a spot on that piece of land to build on. When my mother gave me the ground, I began to work as the dear Lord told me, and to take away the hedge of my mother's field, and to dig out the foundation for a chapel, or a house to worship God in, which was to be called Bethel. Many will have to bless God for ever that Bethel Chapel was built, for many are in heaven already that were born there.*

"In that day there was but one little chapel in our neighbourhood, at a place called Twelveheads, which belonged to the Wesleyans. Our people had a little old house to preach in, which would hold only twenty or thirty people. So we wanted a place to preach in, and the people a place to hear in. Paul had a thorn in the flesh, and so had I. For I had not only the wicked against me, but a little class which was held in the house where we preached.

Most of them turned against me, and tried to set the preachers against me. But with all they could do, they could not hurt me, though they made me uneasy at times.

When I had dug out the foundation of the Lord's house, we had preaching on the foundation stone.

[John Ashworth in Strange Tales Volume 5 published in the 1870s, says Billy stood on the stone and told the people, "If this new chapel, which they say is to be called Bethel, stands one hundred years, and one soul be converted in it every year, that will be one hundred souls – and one soul is worth more than all Cornwall!" Billy then danced on the stone, and shouted "Glory, glory, bless the Lord!" Billy makes a similar statement in his *Journal* referring to Three Eyes Chapel.]

On the day that it was laid, one of our neighbours said he would not give anything towards this chapel. He had two horses that drew the whim at the mine; one of them was taken lame in the field, and lost many days' work. Then the people said that the horse was taken lame because the owner would not give anything to Billy Bray's chapel. But the people must know that it was not mine, but the dear Lord's chapel. And it may be the Lord punished him for not giving anything to his chapel. But the chapel was never much good to that man, for he died very soon after; and the Lord enabled me to build the chapel without his help, bless and praise his Holy Name.

When I had taken down the field hedge, cleared out the foundation, had got some stone home to the place where the chapel was to be built, when the masons had put up some of the walls, and I had £1, 15s. given me by friends, the devil entered into some of my classmates, who said that the chapel ought not to be built there. When my classmates saw that they could not stop me, they went to the superintendent of the circuit and told him that he ought to stop me from building the chapel there, for that was not the place; it ought to be built at Twelveheads or at Tippetts Stamps [Billy has several different spellings for this unidentified place]*.*

Our preacher came to me, and told me that the members had been to him to stop me from building the chapel where I had begun. Then I told him that the Lord had put it into my mind to build the chapel there, and I showed him what I had done already towards building it.

It was the preaching night, and he asked me whether I would be willing to cast lots whether the chapel should be built where I had begun it or in another place. Yes, I said, I was willing; for I did not want to build the chapel there unless it was the Lord's will.

In the evening we went to meeting, and most of our little class were there, and the men who were against me. After preaching, our preacher wrote three lots — for Twelveheads, Tippetts Stamps, and Cross Lanes, which was the place where I had begun my chapel.

When they drew lots, the lot came for Cross Lanes to be the place for the chapel. They then said they would help me to get on with it by raising stone; but talking about it that night was all they did to help me. The following day one of them came to me and said, "We shall not help you, for Cross Lanes did not ought to be the lot." When I have felt so dark, I have said, "Yes, I will build the chapel, my dear Lord." And then I should feel happy again. I write this to let you know that the Lord helped me in building the chapels that I have built, or they would never be built.

So I was as well off as I thought I should be with them. Then I worked away and rose stone and mortar, and put the mason to work. The Lord helped me, for I was very poor and had no money of my own. But the dear Lord rose up friends and sent me money to pay the mason, and we got the chapel walls up, and got timber for the roof and got it sawed and got it up, but we had not timber enough by one sill. So I asked my Heavenly Father to send me some timber or some money to make or buy a sill. That morning there was a Wesleyan local preacher at home praying, and the Lord said to him while he was on his knees, "Go down and give William Bray a pound note."

At that time there was no sovereigns. There was a one pound note on paper. It was drawn on the banks, and was worth twenty shillings. So when the preacher had his breakfast he came down to me by the chapel, and he said to me, "What do you want a pound note for?"

I said unto him, "To buy timber to put up a sill on that end of the chapel."

He said, "I never felt such a thing in all my life. While I was home praying this morning, it was always coming into my mind to go down and give you a pound note. And here it is for you."

So I had the note, and I went to Truro and bought a sill, and put it up on the chapel. And there it is to this day. When the timber was up on the roof, I went around and gathered two pounds toward covering the chapel.

At that time we had children, and the youngest of them was taken very ill. When my little maid was taken ill, Satan tempted me that it would take seven pounds to cover the chapel, and I had but two pounds, and our little maid would die. It would take one pound to bury her, and then I should have but one pound left. The devil tempted me very much on that point. If I wanted it, I had a right to take it, for the dear Lord and me in this place kept but one purse. I paid my money that I got at the mine to the chapel when I wanted it. So I had but one to give my account to, and that was the dear Lord, the very best comrade that man can ever have.

So the devil tempted me that the child would die, and it would take one pound out of the two to bury her. While he was tempting me so sore, for it was sore, it came into my mind, "I shall be paid for building this chapel."

Then it came into my mind, "Yes, because thou hast build this chapel, I will save thy child's life." I said, "Where is this coming from?"

It was said to me, "I am the God of Abraham, Isaac and Jacob. Be nothing doubting. It is me, said the Lord."

I believed it, and it was so. I went home to my house and said to my wife, "Our child [the words "will not" must be missing here in the Journal] die for the Lord told me so."

My wife said, "Do not say so, William. The neighbours say she will die, for she is very bad."

I went to work to the mine, and when I came home the child was not anything better and had not eaten any meat. All that night the child wasn't anything better, and all the forenoon of the following day she was very ill. When I came in to dinner the child was nothing better.

I was afternoon core at the mine, and ever since the dear Lord converted my soul I always felt it my duty to

I Can't Help Praising The Lord

pray with my wife and children before I leave my house to go to work. We knelt to pray, and the child was lying down in the window seat. We had what was very plentiful in that our day, and that was fish and 'taters for dinner.

In my prayer, I said, "My dear Lord, thou hast said that my child shall live, and she have not eat any meat yet."

She begun to eat meat there and then, and she is living now. She is the mother of ten children, and she is well to this day, bless and praise the dear Lord for it. So here the dear Lord made the devil a liar, for I did not want one pound out of the two to bury my child, as the devil said I should. The old devil did not do me any hurt, he only made me the bolder. But I had only two pounds, and the chapel would cost seven.

When the roof was on, I went and borrowed a horse and rode ten or twelve miles from where I lived, up among the farmers. I asked one of them whether he had any reed to sell, for I wanted three hundred sheaves. He told me he had, and it was two pounds for a hundred sheaves. I told the farmer to bring three hundred sheaves to me as fast as he could, and some spears for them. But I did not tell him I had no more than two pounds.

He brought down one hundred at the first and some spears, and I had three pounds when he came. I paid him for the hundred sheaves of reed and the spears. Then I had a few shillings left, and that was all I had. I told the farmer to bring away more reed as fast as he could. I did not tell him I had not money to pay him for it. I had no need to, for before the farmer was a mile off from our place the dear Lord sent a friend with two pounds to me. So as the reed was brought by the farmer, the Lord sent me money to pay him.

I put the thatcher to work to cover the roof, and that cost one pound ten shillings, with a little other work. When he came to be paid I had but one pound, and wanted ten shillings more to pay the thatcher.

There was a high road where a great many people go up and down to work, and dear Lord put it in my mind to go down in the road. I came in the road and the first person I saw was PB.

I said to him, "PB, you have not gave me anything yet towards my father's house."

"No, nor I shall not," says he.

I said to him, "What, are you amind for the Lord to say to you in that day, 'You saw me ahungred and gave me no meat, and saw me athirst and gave me no drink, and a stranger took me not in'?"

He said to me, "I do not care if I do give you ten shillings."

I said, "That is the money that I want."

So he gave me the ten shillings and I went and paid the thatcher. Then I wanted timber for the door and windows, and for the forms. There was a mine, and that mine was stopped, and they was selling off the timber. There was a bargain of timber that would cost one pound six shillings, and I had not money to buy it. A friend came and asked me whether I'd been to the mine and bought any timber.

I told him no, for I had no money. That friend gave me one pound, and with some money the dear Lord sent me from other places I was able to buy and pay the one pound six shillings to the mine and have the timber. Then I wanted the timber brought home to my dear Lord's house, or chapel.

I wanted a horse and cart, and one of our neighbours had a horse. So I went to this neighbour and asked him to lend me his horse. He said to me, "You may have her, but she will not draw anything."

I said, "I will have her and try what she will do."

So I had my neighbour's mare, or horse, and put her in the cart and went away to the mine for the timber. I never saw a better mare in my life. I did not touch her with whip or stick, and we had steep hills to come up over.

So I brought home all the timber, and when I brought my neighbour's mare to him he asked me how she drawed with me.

I told him, "I never saw a better mare in all my life."

Then said he, "I never heard such a thing, for she will not draw with anyone else."

That mare was working that day for a very strong company. If you ask me who they was, they are the Father,

Son and Holy Ghost. Horses, angels, men and devils must obey them. If there was no one there of more power than Billy Bray, the mare would have been as bad with him as she was with others. But bless and praise the name of the dear Lord, he said, "The horse shall work, for the timber is to seat my house." And what the dear Lord say shall be obeyed.

In the counting house of that same mine there was a very large cupboard. It was very large and high. There was an old friend of mine that said, "I will buy that cupboard, for he will do for a pulpit for William Bray's chapel."

There was another man that was a landlord, that said, "And I will buy that cupboard."

Then said my old friend, "That cupboard is for a pulpit in William Bray's chapel. If you buy the cupboard....

[The rest of this line, and the next ten lines, are crossed out and are unreadable, down to the bottom of the page — page 128 in Billy's *Journal*. Maybe Billy did this himself, if he realised he'd got things wrong, or someone else did it because it didn't agree with Bourne's account in which he says the cupboard was bought for Three Eyes Chapel at Kerley Downs. It is clear from the context in Billy's Journal, and also from accounts of the pulpit from Haslam and others, that the cupboard is taken *down* to the chapel, which can only be Bethel. Even Bourne saws it was taken down to the chapel. Kerley Downs is at the very top of the hill. It is likely that when the new Bethel was built, and Billy's original Bethel was turned into a meeting house and school room, that Billy took the pulpit up to Kerley Downs which is where Bourne saw it. Hearing how it was bought, he assumed it had been originally bought for Three Eyes. Here is William Haslam's account of the pulpit/cupboard, which he says he heard directly from Billy.]

It was all done in a humble manner, so that he did not dream of buying any pulpit. One day, as he was passing along the road, he saw that they were going to have a sale at the count house of an old mine. He went in, and the first thing which met his eye was a strong oak cupboard with a cornice round the top. It struck him that it would make a grand pulpit, if only it was strong enough. On examination he found it all he could desire in this respect. He thought if he could take off the top and make a "plat" to stand upon, it would do "first-rate."

He "told Father" so, and wondered how he could get it. He asked a stranger who was there, walking about, what he thought that old cupboard would go for. "Oh, for about five or six shillings," was the reply.

While Billy was pondering how to "rise" six shillings, the same man came up and said, "What do you want that cupboard for, Billy?"

He did not care to tell him, for he was thinking and praying about it. The man said, "There are six shillings for you. Buy it if you will."

Billy took the money, thanking the Lord, and impatiently waited for the sale. No sooner was the cupboard put up, than he called out, "Here, maister, here's six shillin's for un," and he put the money down on the table.

"Six shillings bid," said the auctioneer. "Six shillings. Thank you, seven shillings. Any more for that good old cupboard? Seven shillings. Going, going, gone!" And it was knocked down to another man.

Poor Billy was much disappointed and perplexed at this, and could not understand it at all. He looked about for the man who had given him the six shillings, but in vain. He was not there. The auctioneer told Billy to take up his money out of the way. He complied, but did not know what to do with it. He went over a hedge into a field by himself and told "Father" about it, but it was all clear: "Father" was not angry about anything. He remained there an hour and then went homewards.

As he was going along, much troubled in his mind as to this experience — for he still felt so sure he was to have that cupboard for a pulpit — he came upon a cart standing outside a public house, with the very cupboard upon it, and some men were measuring it with a foot rule.

As he came up, he heard them say, "It is too large to go in at the door, or the window either."

The publican who had bought it, said, "I wish I had not bid for the old thing at all. It is too good to scat up for firewood."

At that instant it came to Billy's mind to say, "Here, I'll give you six shillings for un."

"Very well," said the man, taking the money; "you can have him."

Then Billy began to praise the Lord, and went on to say, "'Father' as good as told me that I was to have that cupboard, and He knew I could not carry him home on my back, so He has found a horse and cart for me. Bless the Lord."

Promising to bring it back very soon, he led the horse down the hill and put the old cupboard into the preaching-house. "There it is," he exclaimed, "and a fine pulpit he does make, sure enough. Now," said Billy, "I want to see thee in it. When will you come." I could not fix for that day, or the next, but made arrangements to conduct a series of services the next week, and promised to have them in that place.

[Billy continues his own account of Bethel:] *Some said I ought to put chembel [a chimney] in my chapel, and some said, "When the chapel is built you shall not have it planned [on the preaching plan]." So I went on and finished my chapel.*

When the Lord's house was finished, some of them said, "Now your chapel is finished you shall not have preaching there." When they said so, I locked up my chapel door and carried the key home to my house and hanged the key to the nail behind the door.

I said, "Lord, there is the key, and I have done what thou hast told me to do. The chapel is built and there is the key. If it is thy will that the key shall stay there for seven years, or thy will that the key shall be taken down every minute in the day, thy will be done, my dear Lord."

That day our preachers planned our chapel more than I should ask if I was there, for they named my chapel and called it Bethel. We had preaching every Sabbath at half past two, six in the evening, and a class meeting in the morning. We got on well there, for the Lord soon revived his work and we had a great many members.

There was a new large chapel built by the old one that

is called Bethel. The old is kept for a school and for class meetings. No wonder for the devil to be against me and put his servants to hinder me from building of Bethel Chapel, for I saw at one time fifteen down asking for mercy, and mercy they had. Some of them is now in heaven praising the dear Lord, and will praise him for ever.

[The "new" Bethel still stands and is in commercial use. All that remains of Billy's original Bethel is a pile of stones in the field opposite. Here is the account of Billy's second chapel — the construction of Three Eyes Chapel at Kerley Downs.]

A little while after I had done building Bethel Chapel, the Lord said to me, "As I have made thee an instrument in my hands of building Bethel Chapel, so I will make thee instrumental in building a chapel at Kerley Downs too."

When the dear Lord said so, I believed it, and I rejoiced greatly to think that I was so honoured to work for so good a master as the King of heaven and earth and sky.

Kerley Downs was near a mile from where I lived and it was in the same parish, the parish of Kea. At Kerley Downs they had their preaching in a dwelling house, and they had a class meeting in the same house, and it was a small one. There was a house near the house they preached in, and it belonged to a widow woman.

Some of the society friends agreed with the woman to buy her house to make it into chapel, and she agreed with them to sell her house. We had preaching there at the woman's house and made a collection, meaning to make the house into a chapel, but they was deceived. After she had agreed with them, someone offered her more money and she let that man have it. And there was no way opened for near twelve months.

About twelve months after, one of the neighbours that had a farm said to one of the class, "Where is that money you collected so long ago to build a chapel and had not done it yet? If your people have a mind to build a chapel, they shall have ground off me."

When the farmer had offered the brother the land to build the chapel, the brother came to me and told me what

I Can't Help Praising The Lord

the farmer had said. Then I went to the friend, for he was a friend and is still. Because he was good to the Lord's cause, the dear Lord is good to he, and that good old friend is living still.

I went to our preacher and told him that we could have a piece at Kerley Downs to build a chapel. I told him if he did not call a meeting and appoint trustees, I would begin about the chapel myself.

So he appointed a day and got trustees, and one man that was at our trust meeting said what he would do. And he never done anything, for I never saw him there until the chapel was built and opened.

We had piece of a hedge to take away before we could clean out the foundations where our chapel was to be built, and before the hedge was taken away all them that promised to help me left me. So my little son and me went on and got some stone, and the good friend that gave us the land to build the chapel let me have his horse and cart to draw stone. He did not charge anything for his horse and cart or land that I know of, but made it a sacrifice to the dear Lord. When my little son and me went on and got stone and mortar, the masons was put to work to build the chapel. We got stone and mede, or clobe as we call it, for the masons to work with.

You that read this must remember that this was not the place where I met, for my meeting house was Bethel Chapel.

I was a very poor man with a wife and five small children at that time, and worked in the mine underground. Sometimes I was forenoon core, and when I had my dinner I should go up to the chapel and work as long as I could see, and then come home and have a little supper and go to bed. Then next day do the same.

The next week I should be afternoon core at the mine, and then I should go up to the chapel in the morning and work until the middle of the day, and go home and away to the mine. And so I did when I was afternoon core, and so I done all that week. The next week I was night core to the mine, and then I worked about the chapel by day and the mine by night. Hadn't the dear Lord strengthened me greatly for his work, I could never have done it. When I was about the chapels I had 'taters to teal [till] in my garden, and every Sunday I was planned. Sometimes I had to walk twenty miles or more, and to speak three times. If I had not the strength from the dear Lord I could not have done it. Many times I have worked twenty hours out of the twenty-four. I remember that when our chapel was up to the door head, the devil said to me in my mind, "They be all gone and left me and the chapel, and I have a good mind to go and leave the old chapel too."

Then I said, "Devil, doesn't thee know me better than that? By the help of the Lord I will have the chapel up, or else I will lost my skin on the downs."

So the devil said no more to me on that subject. Sometimes I have had bladers [blisters] in my hands by working hard, and when I have looked on my hands and saw the bladers, I have said, "I do not mind this, for if this chapel stand one hundred years, and if there is one soul a year converted, that will be a hundred souls in a hundred years and will pay me well if I get to heaven. For they that turn many to righteousness shall shine like the stars for ever and ever. So I shall be rich enough when I get there."

The chapel was built and the roof put on, but we had no money to buy the windows. I went to my neighbours and they was very kind, for they gave me money to buy the windows. There was trustees that belonged to this chapel. Though I had work to do, I had not much to do in getting the money to pay the masons and others. But I collected the money to buy the windows.

So our chapel was built. The opening day came and we had preaching. But the preacher was a wise man but a very dead man, and I believe there was not much good done there that day, for it was a dead time with preacher and people. He had a great deal of grammar but little of Father.

"It is not by wisdom nor by might, but by my Spirit," saith the Lord. And the dear Lord said the truth, for if it was by wisdom or by might I should have a small part. For my might is little and my wisdom is less. Thanks be to the dear Lord the work is his, and he can work by weak instruments.

The second Sunday I was planned there after the chapel was opened, and the Lord was with us and blessed us in a wonderful manner. I said to the people that was there, "You know I did not work here about this chapel to fill my pockets, but to glorify God, and for the benefit of the neighbours, and for the good of souls. And souls I must have, and souls I will have."

Then two women said, "Lord, have mercy on me."

When the women each said so, I said, "Now the chapel is paid for already!"

The Lord worked there, and there was about fifteen members when the chapel was built. The Lord revived his work and soon made them thirty members. Here you can see how good the Lord is to me. I spoke for one soul a year, and he gave me fifteen souls the first year.

Our chapel had three windows, two on one side and one on the other. Then Satan, or the old devil that is no friend to chapels, put his servants by way of reproach to call our chapel Three Eyes, because it had but three windows in it. But blessed be God, the chapel is become too small for that place and it is now made larger. There is six windows now instead of three, and some that have been converted there is now in heaven.

Three Eyes Chapel Kerley Downs after the extension circa 1860, viewed from the north.

[It is ironic that the name 'Three Eyes' a name once used as a form of mockery, has become one of affection. Visitors may like to know that in about 1860 (during Billy's lifetime) when there was a big religious revival in Cornwall, the chapel was extended westward which involved the removal of the western wall to Billy's original chapel, leaving the other three walls intact. Of Billy's three original windows, one was in the eastern wall and the other two in the western wall which had to be removed to enable the extension. It is probable that the latter were then reinstalled in new openings either side of the existing pulpit, as they are of an earlier design (i.e. eight panes over eight) than the other four (with six panes over six). The eastern window was removed and blocked up, leaving the remaining six. There is reliable evidence that Billy preached from the pulpit in the extended chapel during the latter part of his life.]

[Billy built three chapels. The third, Great Deliverance in the village of Carharrack, was opened around 1840. From the following account the work seems to have been well underway in 1838. This time the people are generally supportive, especially the folk at St Ives. Great Deliverance has now been demolished and a house built in its place. Here is Billy's account:]

The dear Lord told me to go and build another chapel, in the parish of Gwennap, and I lived in the parish of Kea. I was instrumental in the hand of the Lord in building two chapels in the parish where I lived: that was Bethel and Kerley Downs chapels. The Lord told me to go in another parish and to build a chapel, and he would help me.

I went to a gentleman, and the Lord opened his heart and he granted me a piece of land to build a chapel, or a house, for the Lord. There was another man that said he would help me get out the foundations and raise stone, and so he did, but he was paid for all he done.

We got out our foundations for building the chapel, and then we wanted a quarry to raise stone. The Lord put it in my heart to go down by the railway, and there we went. Some person had already been there trying to raise stone, but their quarry was poor. They had worked to the east

I Can't Help Praising The Lord

and to the west, and left a piece in the ground in the middle. And there we went to work.

Some wonder at it to see what a quantity of stone I had. But I was working for a strong company. If you wish to know who the company is, I will tell you, my dear friends. It is the Father, Son and Holy Ghost. This company will never break.

I used to work in the mine eight hours out of the twenty-four. When I was forenoon core, and came up at two o'clock, I should have a little dinner and then work in the quarry until that night, and then sometimes go to a meeting. When I was afternoon core I worked in the quarry in the forenoon, and also when I was last core by night.

I was very poor in this world's goods, and had a wife and five children, and I lived a great way off from where I built the chapel. Here the dear Lord helped me again, for he put it in a gentleman's heart to give me five shillings a month while I was raising stone for the Lord's house.

There was a coffee house near our quarry. When I came up from the mine last core by night I would go to the coffee house and have my breakfast for six or seven pence, then pray, and then away to raise stone for the house of my dear beloved Lord. Here you may see that the Lord helped me by giving me my breakfast. You may ask, "How did he help you? You had not anything for building the chapel."

But I was well paid. We have a hundred-fold in this world, and they that turn many to righteousness shall shine for ever, so the more good we can do the greater our reward will be.

We rose away our stone and got it where the chapel was to be built. The foundations was got out, as we thought, forty feet long and twenty-four wide [12.2m and 7.3m]. Then the masons began to build, but I had no money in hand and had no bank to go to but the bank of heaven. But thanks be to God, that is a strong bank. I had often to go there by faith.

When our chapel walls was up about five feet high [1.52m], the man that was with me said, "Our chapel is wider and longer than you say. For he is forty-five feet long [13.7m] and he is wider too. Shall they take down a piece of the end and make it shorter?"

"No," I said. "If the Lord will give us money to cover the short one, he will give us money to cover the long."

And so it was. The Lord sent Mister T to me before the chapel was up, and Mister T said to me, "You will want timber, and lime and slate for your chapel, will you not?"

I said, "Yes, sir, we shall."

He said, "Come down to our store and have what you want for your chapel."

That was the way the dear Lord helped me. When the masons wanted money I went away collecting, and got money to pay them. Some friends was very kind and gave me kind words and money, but some was very rough. I went to one man, and he was well off in this world for he was the manager of the mine. I asked him to give me something to help me build the Lord's house. He was in the mine counting house, and as soon as I asked him he got into a great passion and drove me out. Now that man is dead long ago, and I believe there was no hope in death.

When he drove me out of the counting house, and gave me nothing, I went into a gentleman's house that was nigh by, and asked him for something to help to build the Lord's house. That gentleman said, "Yes, I will give you ten shillings."

I had ten shillings there and then, and that gentleman is living and done well, and he is an old man.

We went around Camborne and some Friends [Quakers] was very liberal. Then we went to the west to a great many places, and I went to Helston.

One of the Friends said to me, "There do a man live in that house that is worth a deal of money. But he is a great miser, and he has never been known to give anything to anyone." I said, "I will go in and see him."

The outside of his house looked like a miser's house, and when I came in there was an old man sitting down to a meal to a little old wisht table. He had an old chair and an old stool or two, and all the clome [earthenware crockery] that I saw was on his table. And that was not much.

So I asked him for something, and he said, "I cannot afford to give you anything."

I said, "You can give me some money, and if you do not you may die and leave it all behind. Job was very rich but he was soon made poor. I am begging for the Lord's house, and if you do not give me some of your money you may die."

Then he wiped his mouth and put hand in his pocket, and took out his hand again. I told him that the gold was the Lord's, and his life was in the Lord's hand and he could take it away, and then the gold would be no good to him.

Then he said, "Go around the town and come again to me by and by."

I said, "You have got money and I must have it now." I talked to him and told him what the dear Lord would do by greedy people.

He wiped his mouth and put his hand in his pocket four or five times and was talking away. At last he put his hand in his pocket and took out two shillings and sixpence and gave it to me. It was a hard job to get the money from that old miser. I do not think Satan let him sleep that night, for the dear Lord helped me take away a half of a crown of his god. I believe money is his god and he love it dearly.

When I came to the Friends, they said, "He have not give anything, have he?"

"Yes," I said, "he gave me two shillings and sixpence."

Then they said, "That is the greatest miracle that was worked in Helston, for he was never known to give anything before now!"

There was a man that lived at St Ives. He was the master of a vessel and he used to come to Penryn and Falmouth. He was called Captain John Havey and he was a teetotal advocate. He and me used to go to the teetotal meetings together.

I used to tell him I was building a chapel [Great Deliverance] for teetotal meetings, and was in debt on the chapel twenty pounds or more for labour to the masons and carpenters. I asked what sort of people St Ives people was, whether they was liberal or no. He said they was, and they gave a deal of money to the cause of God, and they would help me.

My friend told the St Ives people about me, so they knew me before I came there. At that time I had a plan to St Just in the west, and when I had done my work for the Lord in St Just I enquired of a friend my way to St Ives. He told me the way to go and told me who to ask for in St Ives. It was a good man and his name was Bryant.

When I came to St Ives I enquired where my friend Bryant lived, and they told me, "Down by the quay near the sea."

At that time the main street led down on the quay or seashore. St Ives was a very little small place about the year of 1838, but now it is a brave town and greatly improved.

I found my good friend Bryant, and when I told him that I was William Bray he was glad to see me. He asked me how my wife and family was, and they was well. Then I told him what I was come for, and he told me that I was come in a very poor time, for they taken but little fish for the year. There was some of the people almost wanting bread.

He said, "It is a poor time to come to St Ives now."

But he did not know that it was poor times with Peter — till his dear Lord told him to let down the nets on the other side of the ship.

My brother Bryant missed, for I came in a very good time. We went up to the Wesleyan chapel, and there was a great many happy members there. We had a good meeting and prayed for the Lord to send them some fish. After our meeting was over in the chapel we went into the coffee house. After we had a little refreshment we began our meeting and continued until midnight, and we prayed for the dear Lord to send in fish.

When our meeting was over in the coffee house we came out to go to our lodging, and there was the dear and poor women with pilchards on their plates. The fish was shining by the moonlight, for it was a pretty moonlight night. The dear women was smiling, the moon was smiling and we was smiling. And no wonder, for the dear Lord put bread on many shelf that night, and blessed many families.

We asked the dear women what fish was taken. They

I Can't Help Praising The Lord

told us they was ten thousand hogsheads taken in many driving boats, and in some there was twenty thousand taken. The next day, if I make no mistake, there was eight thousand hogsheads taken.

Here I must speak it to their praise. Though they had so much fish in those seas, and the people were so poor, they rested on Sunday and left it till Monday before they went about their fish. And they losed none.

Some men that belong to the fish seine [long nets], said to me, "Now you shall have some money for your chapel. If you can get a boat and come out to our seine we will give you some fish."

There was a carpenter with me and he was used to the sea. He said, "I will bring him out to your seine."

He got a boat and he gave me some clale [probably crail - fishing baskets]. I changed my clothes and he rowed me out to the seine where the fish was. They was looking pretty, for they was shining and leaping about the seine. Then the fisherman dipped up the fish out of the seine, and threw them in the boat where we was. The fish was alive and leaping about our boat, and I thought about the church ministers how they take the tithe of the corn, and I took tithe of the fish.

So when we had done our fishing we came away to land, and there we sold our fish. The carpenter told them up to the people that bought them, and I took the money. The fish money was six pounds fifteen shillings. So the dear Lord helped me as he said he would.

There was another friend that kept a druggist shop. He told me that he would give me all the gain he got by all the medicine that he sell for the week. He gave me two pounds two shillings, so that was well.

The friends in St Ives was very kind, for I had seventeen pounds to bring home. I should have more if I was much about the money, but I was going from one to another telling the people what a good master I had. And who is your master? Why then, that dear Saviour that died upon the cross. Some of St Ives people love that dear Saviour and are with him before now.

So I came home from St Ives with seventeen pounds,

and paid it to the masons and the carpenters. That chapel was built to house our teetotal meetings in, for when teetotalism first came it had many enemies — and it was those that professed religion. Some them would not love a teetotal advocate to come inside their chapel door to advocate that good cause, and some of the preachers would not give it out from the pulpit for a teetotal meeting.

Now here you may see how good the Lord is to me and to the dear neighbours, for the chapel is five feet longer and three feet wider than we meant to build it, and there is a gallery and all. I have seen the chapel full, and some out of doors. If we had built the chapel in our way, it would be too small. But our dear Lord knows better than we.

We had good meetings and class meetings, and we had teetotal meetings. We had some converted in our teetotal meetings, for the dear Lord is able to save souls in teetotal meetings as well as in other meetings, and we have had many blessed times in that chapel.

Great Deliverance Chapel
(now demolished)

Chapter 5

The Prayer of Faith

And the prayer of faith shall save the sick, and the Lord shall raise him up (James 5:15).

I am about, [says Billy] *to write of a woman wherein God's power was made manifest on her in a wondrous manner, and I heard it from her lips twice. I will write down here as near as I can as she told it to me.*

Sister Hoskin was hurted by some way in her thigh so that she was a cripple for seven years, and she was obliged to go on a crutch and a stick. She was so weak that she was forced to drag her foot after her. The doctor said that she would never be sound no more, but the doctor made a mistake, for she was made sound again. He is a God of all power and there is nothing too great for him to do.

She was old when she was converted, and after she was converted some time she felt dark in her mind. I think it was on a Saturday night when she went to bed that she felt very dark in her mind, and she could not sleep. But she prayed to her dear Lord who is able to heal both body and soul, for she wanted a cure for both.

She prayed to her dear Lord, and said in her prayer, "Show me, my dear Lord, whether I am a wheat or a tare."

She prayed away some time like that, and then the cloud broke from her mind and she was made very happy in his love. She said, "Now, my dear Lord, thou hast healed my soul. Why not heal my body, too?"

She meant her sore thigh or leg. When she said so, the Lord said to her, "Arise and go down to my gospel house, and there thou shalt be healed."

She said, "Why can I not be healed here, my dear Lord?" She was in the bed, and it was an easy place for a poor cripple. But when she said so, the dear Lord's Spirit was taken away from her for some time, and she was dark again.

When she found herself like that, she said, "I will go to thy gospel house, or anywhere else, but only let me be healed, my dear Lord."

Then her dear Lord said unto her, "If I heal thee here, they will not believe it. For there is many of them as unbelieving as the Jews was in Jerusalem."

That was true, for if the dear Lord healed her in the bed, many of them would say that she was not healed, for there is many unbelieving people in our country and it is hard to make them believe. But when the dear Lord told Sister Hoskin to go to the chapel, there was many witnesses that saw the almighty power of God in healing that woman.

It was Sunday, so she rosed out of bed to go to the gospel house to get healed, for her faith was strong. But when she got out of her bed and had got downstairs, it was as if the devil stood in the door and tempted her to stop and to have her breakfast first. She said, "No, devil, I will have none. For thee hast many times tempted me to stay for breakfast, and I have had a dead meeting for being so late."

So she left her home with her crutch and stick, and went away for her gospel house, dragging her poor lame foot on the ground. When she came to the chapel it was so early that there was no one there.

When her leader came, he said, "What are you doing here so soon today, Florey?"

Florey said to him, "There is great things going to be done here, for I am going to have a sound leg today, for the dear Lord told me so in the night."

Her class leader told me he thought she was mad, and he said if she had not more faith than he had, she would never have a sound leg. So the meeting began, and while someone was praying, Florey said, "Pray away, the balm is coming."

Then they heard her leg, or thigh, cracking like a stick and she was thrown in the seat. When she rosed up she could walk the chapel without her crutch or her stick.

Some of the people saw her walking the chapel, or gospel house as she called it, at Porthleven. They went around the little town at Porthleven, and said, "Florey Hoskin is

I Can't Help Praising The Lord

walking the Bryanites' chapel with no crutch nor stick."

When the people heard that, a great many came together to see what a miracle the Lord had done. For the dear Lord Jesus Christ had done it, for no one else could never had done such a miracle, bless and praise his Holy Name for ever and ever.

So when the people went out of the chapel, Florey Hoskin rosed and went away without her crutch or stick after being a cripple seven years. When she was going out of the gospel house, one of the people said, "Here, Florey, is your crutch and stick."

Florey said, "You may have they if you will, for I shall not want they any more."

Nor she did not want crutch nor stick any more while she lived in this world. And she do want neither crutch nor stick now, for I believe she is in heaven among the blessed where there is no cripples, and she is no doubt singing to him that loved us and washed us in his own blood, and made us kings and priests to God. Some foolish people will say the Lord do not work miracles in these days like he did in the days of old, but the dear Lord do. If we can believe and pray for it, we are sure to have it.

Florey Hoskin believed, and prayed to her dear Lord that he would hear her, and heal her thigh. She believed that he could do it, and would do it, and he did it according to her faith. She went away from her own house a cripple on a crutch and a stick, with her leg drawn after her, and in a few hours she came home to her own house, and did not want neither crutch nor stick.

Her dear Lord made her a sound woman, so it was well for Florey Hoskin that she served the Lord. It was the same Lord that cured Florence Hoskin that cured the lame man in the days of Peter and John, for he have the same power now as he had then. And what that power is, there do none know, but the dear Lord himself.

[In Billy's *Journal*, his class leader confirms this account in writing.]

[Bourne writes:] At one time Billy had a child seriously ill, whom his wife feared would die. She wished Billy to go to the doctor and get some medicine. He took eighteen pence in his pocket, all the money there was in the house. On the road he met a man who had lost a cow, and was then out begging for money to buy another. His story touched Billy's heart, and to him the money was at once given.

Billy said afterwards, "I felt after I had given away the money that it was no use to go on to the doctor, for I could not have medicine without money, so I thought I would tell my Heavenly Father about it. I jumped over a hedge, and while telling the Lord all about it, I felt sure the child would live. I then went home, and as I entered the door, said to my wife, 'Joey, the child's better, isn't it' 'Yes,' she said.

"The child will live, the Lord has told me so," was his answer, and the child soon got well.

[Bourne tells this about Billy and his wife, Joey:] "My wife said to me one day when lying on her sick-bed, 'William, I do not *see* anything from heaven.' 'Neither do I, and what need has the Lord to show us sights when we can believe without it?'" He continued: "If I saw the Saviour a babe in the manger, I should not believe it more than I do now. If I saw him raise Lazarus out of the grave, I should not believe it more than I do now. If I saw the Lord Jesus raise the ruler's daughter or the widow's son to life, I should not believe it more than I do now. And if I saw the dear Lord nailed to the cross, and heard him cry, 'It is finished,' saw him give up the ghost, and rise from the tomb the third day, I should not believe these things more than I do now."

When he said this, his wife exclaimed, "And so do I believe it," and they both rejoiced together.

This simple faith in God and in his word, what wonders it can accomplish. It is the "secret of power". It is a choice and powerful weapon in the Christian's armoury, which can be used at all times, and never fails. But in dealing with the sick, and those seeking the Lord, it has a special value. Billy spoke of an old man, who had been very wicked, but who was seeking mercy. Billy Bray said to him "You need not fear, for if you ask the Lord for it you are sure to find it. It is said, 'Let the heart of him rejoice that seeketh the Lord,' for they that seek are sure to find him, and when you have found him you will have a good prize."

But the old man did not at once get the blessing, and so Billy continued, "Suppose that you were very poor, and you knew that there was a bag of money in this room, and you were sure that if you sought for it you would find it, and that it would supply all your wants, and you would never be poor anymore; then you would search the room with a *good heart*. The Lord is here, and when you find him you will have all you want."

As this was said, the old man sprung from his seat, exclaiming, "I have got it!" His wife heard him, ran into the room, fell on his neck, both rejoicing exceedingly in the God of their salvation. The old man said, "I never felt anything so 'pretty' in all my life."

"But think how much he lost," was Billy's reflection, "because he did not begin to serve God before." This incident reminds us of another characteristic feature of Billy Bray's life, which may be considered more at length in our next chapter.

Chapter 6

Pure Religion

Then shall the King say unto them on his right hand, "Come, ye blessed of my Father, inherit the kingdom prepared for you from the foundation of the world: for I was an hungred, and ye gave me meat: I was thirsty, and ye gave me drink: I was a stranger, and ye took me in: naked, and ye clothed me: I was sick, and ye visited me: I was in prison, and ye came unto me. . . . Verily I say unto you, insamuch as ye have done it unto one of the least of these my brethren, ye have done it unto me" (Matthew 25: 34-36, 40.)

In this memorable passage from Scripture we are taught that the humblest disciples — the poor, the sick, the despised — are more precious to their Divine Lord than light is to the eye, music to the ear, knowledge to the mind, or love to the heart. The Lord so fully identifies himself with his people, that an injury done to them he reckons as an injury done to him, while a blessing bestowed upon them is a blessing bestowed upon him.

Often dependent himself on the charity of others — for which he was truly grateful — Billy Bray gladly shared with those poorer than himself what little he possessed. He could not keep two hats, one of his friends says, two days, if he knew of a brother in Christ in want of one.

None enjoyed song and prayer and meditation and worship more than Billy; but he never once forgot, in the fullness of his joy, that the naked had to be clothed, and the hungry to be fed. He did not offer to the Lord his God that which cost him nothing. He not only poured out all his heart in devotion to his Saviour, but of his "substance" he willingly took for the Lord's work.

Someone who knew Billy well says, "Many years ago I was holding special services in one of Billy's chapels, making his humble house my temporary home. One morning, after

I Can't Help Praising The Lord

breakfast and prayer, Billy went out, but soon returned with two little children, a boy and a girl, one in each arm. His wife said, 'Billy, where are you going with the children?' He replied, 'The mother's dead, and the father's run away and left them on the stream, and I thought I'd bring them in and rear them up with ours.' His wife remonstrated, saying, 'We have four of our own that you can only just maintain, and these must go to the workhouse.'

[These two children were probably those of Billy's brother James, whose wife died at this time.]

"Billy answered, 'The Lord can as well feed them here as He can in the union,' and the same instant he put them with his own children, saying to them, 'Here, my dears, this is your home now.' His wife was very down-hearted at these two little strangers being thrust upon her, and she having such a small income. I thought Billy had a much bigger heart than myself, as I had a competency and no family, but should have shrunk from the responsibility of bringing up two children.

"I thought I would give Billy something, and found I had £2. 15s. 10d. in my pocket. Seeing Billy's wife Joey in so much distress, I decided to give Billy five shillings towards this maintenance, which, when Billy received, he said, 'There, Joey, the Lord has sent five shillings already, although the children have not eaten a penny loaf;' while I felt as if I had stolen the five shillings, and it was impressed on my mind I had not given enough, and said, 'Here, Billy, give me that five shillings, and taken ten shillings for the children.' Billy replied, 'Praise the Lord! Joey, didn't I tell you the Lord could feed them here as well as in the union?'

"But I became more miserable, and felt I ought to give Billy more; and at last said, 'Here, Billy, the Lord is displeased with me. Give me that half sovereign back and take a sovereign.' He began to praise the Lord, and told his wife to shout 'Hallelujah, for the Lord would provide!'

"I tried to read, but a feeling of wretchedness quite overcame me, and I said, 'Lord, what am I to do?' and the answer was, 'Give Billy more,' so I told him I had not given him enough yet. 'Take another sovereign.'

Billy again shouted, 'Glory be to God! Cheer up, Joey,

the money is coming!'

I then asked the Lord to make me happy, as I had only fifteen shillings and tenpence left, but the impression still was that I ought to give Billy more. I then gave him ten shillings, but could not rest till I had given him all I had. But he refused to take the odd tenpence, saying, 'No, brother, keep that to pay the turnpike gates when you go home.'

"Billy then said, 'Let's have a little prayer,' and while he was praying such a divine power rested on us as I cannot describe, and I never expect such a blessing again this side of heaven. I have been reliably informed that these children were brought up by Billy until they were able to earn their own living."

When he had exhausted his own little store in ministering to the needs of the poor, Billy sought for them help from others. In one instance, a gentleman, to whom he applied, gave him a sovereign for some poor people, and his lady also gave him some clothes for them. After he had had tea, he said he must pray before he left the house, for he felt it as much his duty to pray in a rich man's house as in a poor man's.

The gentleman and lady, with some of their servants, knelt together at his footstool who is "King of kings, and Lord of lords," while Billy poured out all his heart, for he had sweet access to the throne of grace.

Some Quaker Friends, whose kindness to Billy all through life was very marked, were also appealed to, and with the three pounds he collected he bought food and clothing for the family of a "quiet, thrifty, honest man" — and what was a great recommendation to Billy, one who neither drank nor smoked — paid their quarter's rent, filled the cottage with sunshine and gladness, and received himself the blessing of those that were ready to perish.

It seemed strange to Billy that the duty of visiting the sick should be so much neglected. But the unconverted he sought out as well, and his message of mercy in many a sickroom God blessed.

Sometimes young people of good position accompanied him to the house of mourning, and were often greatly blessed themselves, and made a blessing to others.

I Can't Help Praising The Lord

About the same time, Billy found another person whose class leader had been to see her only once in a whole year. He marvelled not that many became therefore indifferent to heavenly things. He was not hopeful about every case. He saw a man who had been very wicked, and was told that he had been seeking the Lord a long time. He said he hoped he had, but added, "It is dangerous to put off our soul's salvation until we are on our deathbed; for where there is one who gets the prize, there are ten who lose it, and the same old devil that got at them downstairs will get at them when they are in their beds."

I well remember having a visit from Billy when, to all appearances, I was on the borders of the grave, and too weak to join in conversation, or to hear other persons talk much. But Billy intermingled, in a very striking manner, prayer and conversation, addressing earnest exhortations to me, with passionate entreaties to Jehovah. He hoped, he believed, he felt sure, that the Lord would raise me up. Then I was exhorted to be faithful, to make full proof of my ministry, to bear a good testimony for Christ always.

Billy burst out into a glowing description of the honours and dignities which in that case should be my reward — I was to have a robe, a palm, a throne, a kingdom, a crown, a crown of glory, a crown of life, a crown of righteousness. Then he interposed the remark — I hardly knew whether it was intended for God or myself, but it nearly convulsed me with laughter — "And I'll wage it will be a fine and pretty one!"

There is no doubt about the brightness of Billy's crown or the fullness of his reward, for in various ways he turned "many to righteousness", and he shall therefore shine forth "like the sun in the kingdom of our Father," or as the "stars for ever and ever."

Chapter 7

Sabbath Keeping

One of the most marked features of Billy's character was his love and reverence for Sunday, the Lord's Day. Before his conversion he had spent his Sabbaths in idleness and sin; afterwards they were sanctified unto the Lord.

[Billy writes:] *At that time we worked in a shaft eight of us together, four cores, two in a core. Our shaft was dry at the bottom where we worked to the ?ninth [nineteenth would be more likely in this account] fathom level, but at the twenty-six there did a stream of water come out of the north wall. There was a fork at that level, and that fork was full in twelve hours. The water was drawn to the surface by a horse whim every twelve hours, and one of we men used to land it.*

It was drawn up Saturday nights at six o'clock, at Sunday mornings at six o'clock, and in the evening at six o'clock. One Sunday out of eight it was my core to land the water.

On the day it was my Sunday to land the water I was at Hicks Mill Chapel. It came into my mind to go to the mine to land the water, and the Lord said unto me, "Stay here and worship me this day."

I said, "I will, Lord."

So I stayed there that Sunday and let the water go to the bottom of the shaft, and it did not hinder no one.

On the Monday morning I went to the mine at six o'clock to land the water. After I had done it, I was going into the other mine. There was two mines there, one was called Cusvey and the other Wheal Fortune, and two captains used to look after both mines. Us worked at Cusvey, and I was going into Wheal Fortune.

I met Captain Hosken coming out, and he said to me, "Where wast thee yesterday, that thee wast not here landing the water?"

I said to him, "It was not the Lord's will that I should come."

He said, "I'll Lord's will thee! Thou shalt not work here anymore!"

When my captain said so, the Lord spoke in my heart. I said, "I have the Lord of rocks and mountains for my friend, and I do not care who is against me."

When I told him so, the power of the Lord came on me so that I shouted for joy. Then he went before me like a man afraid, for "One shall chase a thousand, and two shall put ten thousand to flight."

Then William Roberts, my comrade that worked with me, said, "Captain Hosken hast turned me away too, and you know that it is not my fault."

I said, "No, you shall not be turned away, for it is my fault, not yours. I will go to him with you and tell him."

I said to the captain, "You must not turn away William Roberts, for it was not his fault. It was my core to land the water, not his,"

Then the captain said to me, "That must be done away in thee, for here in the mines we must work Sunday."

I said to him, "I have a new master, and he is a good one, bless and praise his Holy Name. And he tell me that I must not work on the Sabbath day, but keep it holy. I shall do as he tell me, by his help, and shall not work anymore on the Sabbath day."

The clerk that was in the counting house, he was called Mister Mitchel, said, "If I feel like William Bray do, I would not work Sunday neither."

Then the captain said, "Thee should go to work if thou wants."

I said to him, "That is no good, for I shall not work Sundays. Have you any place else to put me to work?"

He said, "Thee may go down to the engine and wheel away the ashes from the engine if you will."

I was glad when he said so, for I could go to meetings or preaching every night. If I was working underground I could not, for us work underground some cores by night.

So I took my wheelbarrow and went to the engine and wheeled away the ashes, and they that I seed I told them what the Lord had done for me. One man cried for mercy, and a revival began at Twelveheads Chapel. I asked the

Lord whether I should go down to Twelveheads or not, and the Lord said to me, "Go."

Whatever people may think about Billy's statements that he heard the voice of God forbidding him to do this, and directing him to do that, or about his belief that God would not allow any harm to be done by the water on the Sunday, surely all must admire Billy's fidelity to his conscience and to God, and his courage in acting up to his convictions of truth and duty, whatever the result might be to himself.

[Billy continues:] *So I left my barrow and the ashes pile, and went away to the chapel. And there I was wanted, for the old professors [of the Christian faith] was very dead at that time, and would come into the chapel with their hats under their arms and look very black on us.*

But the Lord was with us and he tore a hole in Satan's kingdom, for I have seen people crying. The young converts have said to me, "William, there is someone crying. Go and speak to him." And I said, "Let us give a good shout."

We gave a shout and he would fall down, and six or seven more. The Lord would give me power that I could leap for joy when I saw so many fall down and cry for mercy. I think we had nearly a hundred converted in one week, and that was the first week that ever I worked for the Lord. I was twenty-nine years old then, and now I am three score years and ten, and I have the Lord this day in my heart, the hope of glory. Bless and praise his Holy Name for what he done for me and many more.

It was setting day at our mine on Friday that week, our taking day once a month. When I was at Twelveheads Chapel it came into my mind, "I have a good mind to go to the mine as it is taking day, and try to take on." But I said, "No, I will work this week for the Lord."

It was not long after that, in that same day, that two or three men came to the chapel to call me out. They said, "You are going to work with we in Chapels Shaft, for Captain Hosken hast told us to take you with us."

Now this Captain Hosken was the same man that turned me away. So I worked that week for the Lord [at

I Can't Help Praising The Lord

Twelveheads], and we had a blessed week. We had a hundred converted to God, and the revival went on. I may with boldness say that there is many up in heaven praising God now that was converted in that revival, bless and praise his Holy Name.

I went on Monday morning to the mine to see the place that the Lord had got for me, for I believe he got that place for me while I was working for the Lord. It was a good one too.

The miners said, "Bray will be forced to work Sundays now he is gone in Chapels Shaft. For they that sinked from the hundred-and-twenty to the hundred-and-thirty, they have a hundred barrels of water in a core. So Bray is into it now."

But they missed, for the Lord got that place for me. My comrade and me was the first of the pair that begun to work under the hundred-and-thirty. We was eight men and four boys, working six hours a core. Two men and a boy in one core, the boy to draw the stuff, and we was all happy. We always prayed before we went to work, and after we had done. The Lord was with us, bless and praise his Holy Name, for he is good.

So we pecked our shaft, and when the engine was idle the water would come back up through the level and fill up our shaft. As soon as the engine go to work, the water would be all gone again. We did not draw one barrel of water in all the way of sinking to the other level. The place that I was turned away from, because I would not work Sundays, I got about two pounds in a month. In this new place I got five pounds in a month, or more, and I did not work as hard by a great deal as I did before.

So the Lord cleared my way for ever from working Sundays. When I have been going to my plan I have met with the sump shaft men singing for men to go to Capson. They have said to me, "It is no use to press you, for you will not go."

"No," I said, "I shall not go, for I am going to work this day for the Lord."

So I did not lose by serving the Lord, for I got three pounds a month more than I had before, and done the will of the Lord. And that is better than all the money in this world, for: "It is a heaven below, our Jesus to know; and while we do his blessed will, we bear our heaven about us still."

After we had sinked down the shaft to the other level, we went in further east to sink that we call a winze. We began at the same level that we pecked the shaft, and my comrade said to me, "We pecked the shaft and had good luck in the shaft." My comrade was working in a pool of water when he said so. I said, "We shall have good luck in the winze too. For if the Lord would save Sodom and Gomorrah for ten righteous, he will give us a dry winze for two."

By the time the word was out of my mouth my comrade threw in the pick, and down went all the water in a moment. We done well there too, so we can see that the Lord can work miracles as well as in days of old. He is the same Lord, and there is no limits to his power, bless his Holy Name.

A nineteenth century Cornish tin mine

Chapter 8

Trials and Conflicts

Billy came home one payday from the mine without any money. It was a great trial to him, but he bore it meekly. His wife reproached him with being the cause of their poverty and trials, but he said to her, "The Lord will provide," and just then a neighbour, who had heard of his circumstances, came into the house with a basket of provisions containing all that he and his family needed.

When he once took some of the money, that he had earned in the mine, to pay for something wanted for the chapels which he did so much to build, his wife declared, "We shall be brought to the union if you go on in this way."

"Never mind, my dear Joey, the Lord will provide;" and so he did always, often marvellously. Here is one incident from Billy's own lips.

At one time I had been at work the whole of the month, but had no wages to take up when payday came. As we had no bread in the house, Joey advised me to go up and ask the captain of the mine to lend me a few shillings, which I did, and he let me have ten shillings. On my way home I called to see a family, and found they were worse off than myself; for though we had no *bread,* we had bacon and potatoes, but they had neither. So I gave them five shillings, and went towards home. Then I called on another family, and found them, if possible, in greater distress than the former. I thought I could not give them less than I had given the others; so I gave them the other five shillings, and went home. And Joey said —

"Well, William, have you seen the captain?"

"Yes."

"Did you ask him for any money?'

"'Yes; he let me have ten shillings."

"Where is it?"

"I have given it away."

"I never saw the fellow to you in my life. You are enough to try anyone!"

"The Lord isn't going to stay in my debt very long," and I then went out. For two or three days after this Joey was mighty down; but about the middle of the week, when I came home from the mine, Joey was looking mighty smiling, so I thought there was something up.

Presently Joey said, "Mrs. So-and-so has been here today."

"Oh?"

"And she gave me a sovereign."

"There, I told you the Lord wasn't going to stay in my debt very long; there's the ten shillings, and ten shillings interest!"

Coming home one Sunday evening from his preaching appointment through a dirty road, Billy stuck in the mud, and in extricating one foot he tore off the sole of his shoe. Holding it up, now almost useless, he said, "Here, Father, thou knowest that I have worn out these shoes in thy cause, and I have no money to buy new ones. Help me."

The Lord heard him in this time of need, and sent speedy relief. A friend the next week said he wanted Billy to accompany him to Truro. On their arrival he took him first to a shoe shop, and bought for him a pair of shoes, and then to other shops to get some needed articles of clothing.

Billy was very poor when he was converted. A low-priced dark heavy cotton jacket was his best, and he said that was better than he deserved; but shame from wearing poor clothing did not stop him from going out on the Sunday to warn his fellow-men to "flee from the wrath to come." At the request of a servant girl, an unknown Quaker Friend gave him a coat and waistcoat, "which suited me," he said, "as if they were made for me; and they served me for years."

[Billy writes:] *It is many years since I heard my [Christian] brother tell this tale at a missionary meeting, but I will tell the tale that he told, as near as I can. If I miss, I do not mean to. Sometimes, he said, after he had done preaching he had no place to lodge for the night, and nothing to eat, poor dear man. I think he said that he have been out in a cold frosty night, and when he have awaked in the morn-*

ing, after being out all night, he have been so cold that he have been forced to blow his breath and keep his hands by his mouth for a great while before he could get any heat into himself.

When this brother's clothes got poor the devil tempted him, and said, "Now see how the Lord hath served thee, for thy clothes is just done. And what wast thee do then?"

But he trusted his dear Lord, and the Lord opened the heart of a friend. I believe it was a Quaker Friend that asked him one day, "Is that all the clothes thee hast got?"

And he said, "Yes."

Then the good Friend said, "Thee come to my house and I will give thee some clothes." He told him where he lived and when to come.

The brother went to the good Friend's house as he promised, and the good Friend told him to strip off his old clothes and to put up his new. So our brother did, and he was glad to do so.

After he had his clothes, my dear brother said, "Now, devil, see how the Lord have opened my way, and how I am dressed now."

Then said the devil, "Now thee hast no meat."

In a small span of time the dear Lord opened another heart, and that person sent him money. Then the brother said, "Now, devil, I chase thee all over this mission with penny loaves and water!"

You can see by what our brother said that he loved souls, and he did not look for a high life. He would live on bread and water to be instrumental in the hand of the dear Lord of saving blood-washed souls.

He was made a great blessing in the hand of the Lord in that place, and to that neighbourhood. Many will have to praise God in heaven that ever that dear brother went to that place, for it was a wicked place before he went there. They carried on all sorts of wickedness, but he was an old man and cared for no man. He preached Christ and salvation, and hell and damnation, and the word was with power, for many heard and turned to the Lord.

Now who can tell the value of that suit of clothes that Quaker Friend gave to that preacher? No doubt but this was the best suit of clothes that he ever gave in all his life, and his dear Lord will reward him for that great kindness, if that Quaker Friend is on the right ground. But we must be born again, or there is no reward for us.

If we give our goods to feed the poor and our bodies to be burnt, if we have not charity it will not avail nothing. That charity that the apostle [Paul] speak of is the love of God in the heart. If we have his love in our heart, then bless and praise his Holy Name, every promise is sure. The Lord's word is true, "Heaven and the earth shall pass away, but my word shall never pass away."

May the dear Lord bless them, is the prayer of William Bray. I know this preacher well, and I have been to missionary meetings with him and to other meetings too. We have had many good meetings together, and have been very happy, bless and praise the dear Lord for he is good, and he is very kind to all them that love him. And I am glad that I do love him.

It was Billy's belief that the Lord opened the hearts of his friends to help him whenever he needed it, and shut them up when help was no longer required.

Billy had other trials in his family besides those of which we have spoken. He had two sisters, and one of them, who was out of her mind, was very trying. She was sometimes so cross that she exercised Billy's faith and patience more than a little. But he had one unfailing resort in trouble. "I cried to the Lord, and he heard me, for he made me so happy that I could not hold it in. I had a joy unspeakable and full of glory. I had good measure, pressed down, and running over. Now what was that trial compared with the blessing I received? I was so happy that I felt none of these things could move me. I could say, 'I long to be with Christ now. My dear Lord, let me die, and take me to heaven.' I felt so much of the Divine glory that I longed to be there. I cannot tell what I felt."

Did he not know what the Saviour meant when he said, "In the world ye shall have tribulation; *but be of good cheer,* I have overcome the world?"

And yet one other kind of trial we must mention. During his

I Can't Help Praising The Lord

wife's long illness, which ended in her death, Billy said he "had many blessed seasons while praying with her, and promises, from the dear Lord." At one time the words, "She is mine for ever," were so deeply impressed on his mind that tears came into his eyes.

Billy said that the devil tempted him with these words. "Well, I'll have thee down to hell after all."

But Billy said to him, "I'd as soon go to hell with thee as not. For I'd bring Jesus Christ with me, and shout and sing, and praise the Lord!"

If temptation came with the thought that he was a fool to go and preach, as he would never get anything for it, the answer to the devil was, "Not so big a fool as thee art, for once thee was in a good situation, and did not know how to keep it!"

A graphic account of how Billy "beat the devil" when his crop of potatoes failed, is so good, that we gratefully insert it here.

"Friends, last week I was a-diggin' up my 'taturs. It was a poor yield, sure 'nough; there was hardly a sound one in the whole lot. And while I was a-diggin' the devil come to me, and he says, 'Billy, do you think your Father do love you?' 'I should reckon he do,' I says. 'Well, I don't,' says the old tempter in a minute.

"If I'd thought about it I shouldn't have listened to him, for his opinions ben't worth the leastest bit of notice. 'I don't,' says he, 'and I tell 'ee what for: if your Father loved you, Billy Bray, he'd give you a pretty yield of 'taturs; so much as ever you do want, and ever so many of 'em, and every one of 'em as big as your fist. For it's no trouble to your Father to do anything; and he could just as easy give you plenty as not, and if he loved you, he would, too.'

"Of course, I wasn't goin' to let him talk of my Father like that, so I turned round upon him. 'Pray, sir,' says I, 'who may you happen to be, coming to me a-talking like this here? If I'm not mistaken, I know you, sir, and I know my Father, too. And to think of you coming a-saying he don't love me! Why, I've got your written character home at my house; and it do say, sir, that you be a liar from the beginning! And I'm sorry to add, that I used to have a personal acquaintance with you some years since, and I served you faithful as any poor wretch could; and all you gave me was nothing but rags to my back, and a wretched home, and an aching head, and no 'taturs, and the fear of hell-fire to finish up with. And here's my dear Father in heaven. I have been a poor servant of his, off and on, for thirty years. And he's given me a clean heart, and a soul full of joy, and a lovely suit of white as'll never wear out; and he says that he'll make a king of me before he've done, and that he'll take me home to his palace to reign with him for ever and ever. And now you come up here a-talking like that.' Bless 'ee, my dear friends, he went off in a minute, like as if he'd been shot — I do wish he had — and he never had the manners to say good morning!"

Billy knew, too, how to fight the devil and his agents with their own weapons. Returning late from a revival meeting, on a dark night, in a lonely road, some men tried to frighten him by making all sorts of unearthly sounds; but he went singing on his way. At last one of them said, in the most terrible tones, "I'm the devil up here in the hedge, Billy Bray."

"Bless the Lord! Bless the Lord!" said Billy, "I did not know thee wost so far away as that!" To use Billy's own expression, "What could the devil do with such as he?"

At a friend's house in Truro the mistress read the account of the temptation of our Lord at family prayers. Billy listened quietly till the verse was read in which Satan promises the Saviour all the kingdoms of the world, and the glory of them, if he would only fall down and worship him. Then Billy jumped to his feet exclaiming, "The old vagabond! The old vagabond! He give away all the kingdoms of the world when he never had an old 'tater skin to call his own, the old vagabond!"

Chapter 9

Drinking and Smoking

What? know ye not that your body is the temple of the Holy Ghost which is in you, which ye have of God, and ye are not your own? For ye are bought with a price: therefore glorify God in your body, and in your spirit, which are God's (1 Corinthians 6:19-20).

Any life of Billy Bray would be considered by all who knew him as incomplete that did not refer to his strong detestation of taking intoxicating drink, and of smoking. He had been much debased by drunkenness, and had been a perfect slave to the pipe.

[There were many temperance societies operating at the time in Cornwall, mostly connected to chapels, in which the Bible Christians played a major part.]

"When I heard," Billy says, "that Mr. Teare was coming to Hicks Mill to lecture on teetotalism, I thought I would go to hear him, but that I would not sign the pledge; for a little drop, if a man does not take too much, will do him good. As I listened to what Mr. Teare had to say, the darkness was removed from my mind, and I thought I would sign the pledge. Before Mr. Teare had finished speaking, I shouted out to friend Tregaskis, 'Thomas, put down my name!"

From that hour Billy was not only a staunch teetotaller, but also one of the most earnest and successful advocates of the great cause of temperance.

But Billy used to say "If Satan ever catches me, it will be with the ale pot. Men set lime-sticks to catch birds, and Satan sets wine bottles and ale pots to catch fools, but I will not touch a drop, then I shall never get drunk." The same idea sometimes was applied more widely, as when he said, "If you are a little greedy or poor-tempered, the devil will get in his nail, and pinch thee tight!"

At one temperance meeting, speaking of moderation,

Billy said, "Ye might as well hang an old woman's apron in the gap of a potato field to prevent the old sow with young pigs from going in, as expect a drunkard to be cured with moderation. Satan knows that, so he sets the little pot to catch him again."

Billy also fully endorsed the opinion which he had heard expressed, that public houses were hell houses. He knew one house where nineteen men got drunk, and while in a state of intoxication fell into mine shafts, and were killed. "Hell houses," he would say, "indeed they are! For they are places where people are prepared for hell, and they help people on their way." But with his love of antithesis, and his habitual cheerfulness, even "hell-houses" reminded him of chapels, where people are converted and prepared for heaven, and therefore might properly be called "heaven houses."

I well remember how wisely and faithfully, yet lovingly, he dealt with a professing Christian who had fallen through drink. Billy and I spent nearly a whole day in talking to the unhappy victim, and in praying with and for him. He was, we believed, mercifully restored to God's favour, and could again humbly trust in his mercy. But Billy told him he must be on his guard against his besetting sin, and keep beyond the length of the devil's chain.

[Billy said:] A crafty fox down their way had managed, though chained, to devour some foolish chickens. A few grains of corn he had kicked a long distance away, which were speedily picked up by the chickens, without thought of danger. Then a few more, but not quite so far off. Then a few again a little nearer, and then a little nearer still, till the unsuspecting birds came within reach, when he at once sprang upon them and devoured them.

"Satan would serve him like that," explained Billy. "Only one glass, *that* he might take without danger; two glasses even, and yet be quite safe. He might think, perhaps, he could take three or four; but if he got on such dangerous ground he was putting himself in the devil's power, and he would drink till he got drunk again, and then the devil would say, 'That is your religion, is it? You may as well give up your hopes and professions at once. No one will believe in you any? more; I have you completely in my power, and you shall not escape.'"

Billy's view on smoking we cannot lightly pass over without being unfaithful to his memory. [He writes,] *"I was, before I was converted, a smoker as well as a drunkard. I used to smoke and I loved smoking almost as well as I loved my meat, and would rather go down in the mine without my dinner than without my tobacco and pipe. But now I have a new master, better than tobacco and pipes. Everyone in Christ Jesus is a new creature; old things is passed away and all things is new.*

In the days of old the Lord spoke by the mouth of his servants the prophets, but now he speaks in our hearts by the Spirit of his Son. So I had not only the believing part, but I could hear the small still voice within that speaks to me. When I would take the pipe to smoke, it would be applied within, "It is an idol, a lust. You are lusting after an idol and I want you to give it up and to worship me with your whole heart."

For so it was, and when I used to put a little tobacco in my mouth it would be said to me, "Worship me with clean lips."

Then I would take the tobacco out of my mouth and throw it on the ground. And after a little time I might forget, and put some in my mouth again, but as soon as it was in my mouth it would be, "Worship God with clean lips."

The Lord told me it was not right to smoke nor chew, but this did not do, so he sent a woman called Mary Hook to convince me. I went into a house and took the pipe out of my pocket and went to light it. And Mary said to me, "I see that you smoke. Do you not feel [presumably bad — or guilty] from smoking?"

"Yes, I feel something inside telling me that it is an idol and a lust."

She said with a very loud voice, "That is the Lord."

Then I said, "Now I must give it up, for the Lord is telling me of it inside, and the woman outside. So the tobacco must go, love it as much as I will."

So there and then I took the tobacco out of my pocket

and threw it in the fire, and put the pipe under my foot and said, "Ashes to ashes, dust to dust."

Thanks be to God I have not smoked since, and that is forty-one years ago now. But I found old habits hard to be broken, and I was forced to pray mightily to the Lord and ask him for help. Bless his Holy Name, he helped me. The Lord said, "Cry to me in the time of trouble and I will deliver you." And I was the man that wanted help.

So I asked the Lord for strength against that habit, for it is a bad one, and it is not everyone that can give it up, for it do enslave a man. It takes a firm mind to conquer that, and then he must ask for help of the Lord."

It was especially pleasing to Billy if he could persuade young men to imitate his example. He would tell them that the pipe was no help to them in the way to heaven, but an enemy to body and mind and pocket. When the good Spirit suggests to the mind of a good man to read a chapter in the Bible, the evil spirit which is after the flesh will say, "I would have a pull at the pipe first;" and by the time he has fit his pipe and smoked, something comes along for him to do, and he does not read at all for that time. When it comes into his mind to pray, it is said, "I would have a pipe first;" and by the time the pipe is done, something comes in his way that calls him off; and there is no praying for that time. The pipe has robbed the Christian of hundreds of chapters and prayers, besides proving injurious in point of health and wealth.

Billy was particularly hard upon some preachers. Billy and a preacher of somewhat the same type of character were holding a missionary meeting. Billy opened the meeting with prayer, and the preacher and others fervently responded to many of his petitions. Observing this, he began to be more detailed and pointed in his requests. "O Lord, help the people to give up their idols."

The preacher said, "Amen."

"May thy children be saved from the love of the world's fashions."

"Amen," again said the preacher.

"Help thy people to give up their ribbons and feathers."

"Amen," was still the response of the preacher; and

again "Amen" when he added, "And their cups and drinks."

"And their pipes and tobacco," but to this there was no "Amen" from the preacher.

Billy at once said, "Where's your Amen, Brother? Why don't you say 'Amen' to the pipes as well as the cups? Ah, you won't say 'Amen' to the pipes!"

Billy then proceeded with his prayer. But the preacher afterwards found fault with him for thus rebuking him in public. Billy justified himself by saying, "You were hearty and loud enough with your 'Amens' for others to give up *their* idols; but you are not willing to part with your own. Bless the Lord, I have given up *all* for my Saviour."

Chapter 10

Rebuke and Exhortation

Billy's wonderful tact and choice of words in speaking to friends and strangers personally, was certainly one of the most marked features of his character. He had such an insight into people, he had such a sense of times and seasons, he had such a power of putting the truth in an available form, that men could take it without hesitation, and digest it, as it were.

Billy seemed to be one of those unordained men that are ordained of God from their birth to be teachers in this way. His heart seemed to take such hold of people that it led him to think about them, and pray for them, and brood over them with the tenderest, purest affection and sympathy.

But his talents were multiplied by the wise and benevolent use he made of them; and to people who say, "I have not the power he had; and if I had I should not know how to use it," it may be said, as has been said in a similar case, "But it does not follow you ought not to learn; for the *learning* is very essential." The Church needs the power to preach to individuals, and to preach, as did her Divine Lord, her best sermons, too, on such occasions.

An old gentleman once took great umbrage at Billy's faithful reproofs and lively manner in giving prominence to Divine things in everyday life, and at last he became full of hatred to one who strove to acknowledge God in all his ways. But when affliction overtook him, and death and judgment and eternity appeared close at hand, he found that his lamp gave neither light nor warmth.

On Billy's entering the sick chamber, looking around on the costly furniture, he spoke aloud, and yet as if he were speaking to himself, "Did Jesus Christ ever occupy such a fine place as this, or spend money to gratify fleshly desire and worldly taste?" Then in a strain of tenderness and pity, he began to commiserate Jesus on his deep poverty, while sojourning here below, till the bystanders were annoyed, and the old gentleman flushed with indignation and wrath.

But when Billy had as he thought probed the wound enough, he applied the healing balm. And while he was praying, a sweet peace stole over the sufferer's mind and greatly comforted his troubled heart. Billy was now asked to stay with the sick man until his departure hence, which was not till two or three weeks afterwards. Billy had some of the sorest conflicts he ever experienced during that time, but in every instance he came off victorious through the blood of the Lamb. He was more than a conqueror through him that loved him.

The old gentleman, too, again and again lost his hold of God, but Billy as often rendered the help which the poor man so much needed. He kept him whom he had under his care in contact, as it were, with the truth, and the Spirit, and the Saviour, till his mind underwent a complete transformation. At last he could no longer doubt that the day of eternal brightness and joy had dawned, for "the day-star had arisen in his heart." The light of "the city that hath no need of the sun" shone all around, and without a cloud he passed away to his home in the skies.

Billy left the house early one summer's morn, with the last practical proof of the old gentleman's gratitude in his pocket, when he met an absent son from a distance on his way to see his father. To his inquiry how he was, Billy joyfully answered, "Never so well in all his life, for he is just gone off with the beautiful shining ones!"

In January 1867, Billy went to Plymouth and Devonport to hold some meetings for the Primitive Methodists, for he was willing to serve all to the best of his ability, because he loved all them that loved the Lord Jesus Christ in sincerity. They had blessed meetings, rather noisy too. A man reproved Billy in the street for making so much noise. Billy spoke very sharply and said he did not mind who heard him. He was not ashamed to do his Master's work out in the street, and those who loved the Lord ought not to be ashamed to praise him in the chapel.

Said Billy, "I told the man that I did not fear him, nor his master, the devil; and if I had hearkened to such as he I should have lost my best Friend long ago. My best Friend is the dear Lord. He has made me *glad,* and no one can make me sad. He makes me shout, and there is no one who can make me doubt. He it is that makes me dance and leap, and there is no one that can keep down my feet. I sometimes feel so much of the power of God that, I believe, if they were to cut off my feet I should heave up the stumps!"

Billy was emphatically a *happy* Christian; he rejoiced in the Lord *always.* His friend Mr. Haslam questioned him on one occasion as to the secret of his *constant* happiness, comparing Billy's experience with his own. He was not always, Mr. Haslam said, on the Mount. His prospects were sometimes clouded. At times his fears rather than his faith prevailed; he therefore wanted to know how it was that Billy got on so much better than he did. Billy answered that we must become fools for Christ's sake; that Christians, like Mr. Haslam, who had so much book-larnin', having so much to unlearn, were placed at a disadvantage when compared with some others, "For some of us, you know," Billy added, "are fools to begin with!"

On most occasions, Billy's wit sparkled and flashed without effort apparently on his part. But he knew how to hold it in reserve when people sought merely to gratify their curiosity, or wished him to display his powers for their amusement. Some such got more than they bargained for. Thus, to a lady who once spoke with him for this purpose, he was very silent and reserved.

She, hoping to draw him out, said, "You know we must be willing to be fools for Christ's sake."

"Must we, ma'am?" was his ready answer. "Then there is a pair of us!"

Reproached one day by a depraved, dissolute man, as being one of those idle fellows who go about living upon others, and doing nothing whatever, he said, "My Father can keep me a gentleman always if he pleases, without my doing any work at all; but your father" — pointing to his shabby tattered garments — "cannot even keep you in decent clothes with all your hard work!"

Chapter 11

Fully Ripe for the Garner

It might be thought that a man who had so given himself up to the public, must have *neglected,* in some measure, his own family and friends. But wife, children, brother, mother, uncle, and other relatives, believed because of his word, and had the great reward of faith in the blessing of a joyful experience, already forming quite a large group in the kingdom of eternal glory.

Billy always enforced the principle that the "best" should be given unto the Lord, and not the "blind", the "lame", or the "sick". At one time at a missionary meeting he seemed quite vexed because there was something said in the report about money received for "rags and bones". And when he rose to address the meeting, he said, "I don't think it is right, supporting the Lord's cause with old rags and bones. The Lord deserves the best, and ought to have the best. However, he is very condescending, for when a person has a little chick that is likely to die, puts it into a stocking and lays it by the fire, saying, 'If that chick lives, I will give it to the missionaries,' it is not long before it says, 'Swee, swee, let me out, I am better.'

"I knew a woman down at St. Just some years ago who had two geese, and though she might have a good flock to begin, she could never rear above two or three. At last she promised the Lord if He would increase her flock she would give every *tenth* goose to the missionaries. Now I reckon," Billy continued, "you will say that that woman had a good heart; but I don't think so, for if she gave every *fifth* goose to the missionaries she would have then more than she had before! However, the Lord took her at her word, and the next year she had *eleven,* and they all lived till they grew up nearly as big as old ones. And then the Lord tried her faith; one of her geese died. And what do you think the devil said? *'That's the missionary goose!'*

"That's how the devil would serve the missionaries. He would give old, dead, stinking geese to them to eat, but what do they want of an old, dead, stinking goose? But she knew him, and she said, 'No, devil, I have ten left now, and the missionaries shall have one of them.' And the next year she had eleven again. They were out swimming about the pond, with their great long necks and their beautiful white feathers; they were the most respectable-looking geese I ever saw."

An old Independent minister, who had kindly lent his chapel for a meeting, sitting by my side, said to me at once, "I suppose you would not like to vouch for the soundness of his theology." And before I had time to answer, Billy was in the midst of an illustration of his meaning that set us all in laughter. He said he knew a young man once who had been very wicked, and when convinced of his great sinfulness by the Spirit of God, he despaired for a long time of finding mercy.

Billy among others tried to comfort him; but to all they said he only answered, "As I have never done anything for the Lord, I have not, I really have not, got the cheek to ask him to bestow on me so great a blessing as the forgiveness of my sins." But the thought, later, that he had once given five shillings to help on the Lord's cause, at a time when help was much needed, greatly encouraged him. Billy said his gift "did not make the Lord a bit more willing to save him, but it made *him* more willing to be saved;" and therefore Billy believed "the devil kept the thought out of the young man's mind as long as he could."

I remember being with Billy once on a mission, when some well dressed people ashamed, I suppose, to be seen putting coppers into the plate, put in some peppermints. Some of them followed us to the meeting in another place the next night, and Billy said that formerly plain, poor women, had such love for the cause, that they would make great sacrifices often to give a silver shilling. And each of them was he said, worth a dozen penny ladies, or twenty-four half-penny ladies, and he did not know how many of the peppermint ladies that came sometimes to their meetings; and he believed some of this class were then present!

I Can't Help Praising The Lord

It is important to speak of Billy's deep piety, his abiding sense of the Divine favour, the secret of his great usefulness, the source of his constant and perpetual joy. The "much fruit" which is so pleasing to God cannot come except the roots have struck deep into the soil. Religion is not shallow in its nature. "The water that I shall give you," said the Saviour, "shall be in you a *well of water* springing up into everlasting life."

To be "sanctified wholly", to use an apostolic phrase, Billy very early in his religious history felt to be both his duty and privilege.

[Billy writes:] *I remember being at Hicks Mill Chapel one Sunday morning at class meeting when a stranger led the class. The leader asked one of our members whether he could say that the Lord had cleansed him from all sin, and he could not.*

"That," I said in my mind, "is sanctification. I will have that blessing by the help of the Lord." And I went on my knees at once, and cried to the Lord to sanctify me wholly, body, spirit, soul. And the Lord said to me, "Thou art clean through the word I have spoken unto thee." And I said, "Lord, I believe it."

When the leader came to me I told him, "Four months ago I was a great sinner against God. Since that time I have been justified freely by his grace, and while I have been here this morning, the Lord has sanctified me wholly."

When I had done telling what the Lord had done for me, the leader said, "If you can believe it, it is so." Then I said, "I can believe it." When I had told him so, what joy filled my heart I cannot find words to tell. After meeting was over, I had to go over a railroad, and all around me seemed so full of glory that it dazzled my sight. I had a joy unspeakable, and full of glory.

One of the most blessed results of Billy's deep piety was his *unfeigned humility*. His estimate of himself in comparison with other Christians was that he was a coarse crystal among beautiful specimens.

At public meetings the idea would sometimes come out

in a somewhat different fashion. The several speakers, and their brilliant, eloquent, and powerful speeches, reminded him of the precious stones with which the foundations of the heavenly Jerusalem were adorned, but the greatest wonder was that God, after having hewn these out of different quarries, and made them polished stones in his glorious temple, should pick up "an old Cornish Crystal" to set off their great and manifold excellences with still greater effect.

His humility was his safeguard all through life. [Billy writes,] *Soon after I was converted, the devil said to me, "Billy Bray, you'll be a great man." But I sunk into nothing, and in that way slipped through the devil's hands.*

Another result of Billy's deep piety was his *continual sense of dependence upon God*. The Lord's servants without the Lord's presence are weak like other men, like Samson when he lost his locks. Here is one experience of Billy's [although not from his *Journal*]. When I was in the St Neot Circuit, I remember one Sunday I was planned at Redgate and there was a chapel full of people. The Lord gave me great power and liberty in speaking, but all at once he took away his Spirit from me, so that I could not speak a word — and this might have been the best sermon that some of them ever heard!

"*What*," you say, "looking like a fool, not able to speak?"

Yes, but it was not long before I told them, "I am glad I am stopped, and that for three reasons. The first is to humble my soul and make me feel more dependent on my Lord, to think more fully of him and less of myself.

"The next reason," I told them, "is to convince you that you are ungodly. For you say we can speak what we have a mind to, without the Lord as well as with him. But you cannot say so now, for you heard how I was speaking. But when the dear Lord took away his Spirit I could not say another word. Without my Lord I can do nothing.

"And the third reason," I said, "is that some of you young men who are standing here may be called to stand in the pulpit some day, as I am. The Lord may take his Spirit from you as he has from me, and then you might say, 'It is no good for me to try to preach or exhort, for I was stopped the last time I tried to preach, and I shall preach no more.'

"But now you can say, I saw poor old Billy Bray stopped once like me. He did not mind it, and he told the people that he was glad his dear Lord had stopped him. And Billy Bray's dear Lord is my Lord, and I am glad he stopped me too. For, if I can benefit the people and glorify God, that is what I want.'" I then spoke a great while, and told the people what the dear Lord gave me to say."

Billy kept the great object of life before him wherever he went, whatever he did. Thus he writes [but not in his *Journal*], "I was asked to go to the reopening of a chapel. We had large congregations. I spoke in the forenoon, and brother Coles spoke in the afternoon and evening. He had the mighty power of God, and preached two very good sermons. The people were very kind in giving their money for repairing God's house. On the Monday they had a tea meeting, and I had to speak at three o'clock. The tea was at five. I believe we should be better off if we were to *fast,* and *pray,* and give the money without a tea; we should have more of the glory in our souls. In the evening we had a speaking meeting.

"One of our friends took the chair. He called on the superintendent to speak first; and after that he called on me. I told the people that the dear Lord had given them a pretty chapel to worship in; and now he wanted good furniture, for bad furniture looks disgraceful in a good house. I told them that good furniture for the house of the Lord was *sanctified souls.* We must be pardoned, sanctified, and sealed, and then we shall not only be fit for the Lord's house on earth, but *we shall be good furniture in heaven.*"

One of Billy's last written records, [again, not in his *Journal*] as late as February 10th, 1868, was, "In the morning after I had breakfast, bad as I was, I thought I would go to see some friends; and after calling on some of them, I went home. But I had hard work to get home, I was so ill; and my breath was short."

Only a little earlier, he had been at Newlyn [Newlyn East, near Newquay] and Crantock, labouring among the Wesleyans. There was a revival in progress in the latter place, and in a revival Billy was always at home. "The dear Lord made the people very happy, and me happy with them." After the meeting in the chapel was closed one night, many of the people adjourned to a friend's house. There some were singing, some praising God, and others crying for mercy. Six souls were set at blessed liberty, and the meeting was continued till a very late hour.

"We could do nothing but praise," Billy said, "for the Spirit was poured out in such a wonderful manner. I was as happy as I could be and live. It was one stream of glory." He was very weak in body then, but as the outward man decayed, the inward man was renewed day by day. "I think I shall be home to my Father's house soon," was his happy thought, his glorious hope. He returned home pale and exhausted.

He left it but once afterwards, when he went to Liskeard to see his children. He got much worse, and appeared like a man in the last stage of consumption. On one occasion he sent for a medical man, and when he arrived he said, "Now, doctor, I have sent for you because people say you are an honest man, and will tell them the truth about their state." After the doctor had examined him, Billy said, "Well, doctor, how is it?"

"You are going to die."

Billy instantly shouted "Glory! Glory be to God! I shall soon be in heaven." He then added in a low tone, and in his own peculiar way, "When I get up there, shall I give them your compliments, doctor, and tell them you will be coming too?" This, the doctor says, "Made a wonderful impression upon me."

It scarcely need be said that Billy retained all his old love for shouting. He even said if he had his time to go over again he would shout ten times as much. In his affliction he was visited by Christians of all denominations, who liberally contributed to his support. On Friday, May 22nd, 1868, he came downstairs for the last time.

To one of his old friends, a few hours before his death, who asked if he had any fear of death, or of being lost, he said, "What? Me fear death? Me, lost? Why, my Saviour conquered death. If I were to go down to hell, I would shout glory, glory, to my blessed Jesus, until I made the bottomless pit ring again, and then miserable old Satan would say, 'Billy, Billy, this is no place for thee: get thee back.' Then up to heaven I should go, shouting, 'Glory, glory, praise the Lord!'"

Billy took his departure to be with the Lord on Monday, May 25th, 1868, having reached the age of seventy-four years within a few days.

On the Friday following, a large number of his friends and neighbours assembled at his house. When the coffin was brought out into the yard, two appropriate addresses were delivered, one by Mr. JD Balkwill, Billy's pastor, and the other by Mr. Thomas Hicks, an old and much attached friend. His remains were interred at Baldhu Church.

If Billy Bray had not been a Christian, he had been nothing; and the mere *form* of religion, with which many are easily satisfied, would have utterly failed to comfort and support him in his trials and temptations. Billy was so greatly honoured and blessed himself, and made so great a blessing to many, because his faith was a glorious reality — part and parcel of his daily life and experience. He lived out in his life the teaching and promises that he believed in his heart.

Billy's grave at Baldhu today